WOMAN
BE WILD

*The Path To Feminine
Awakening, Empowerment,
& Freedom*

Vol. 2

— Indigo

Cover Art and Sacred Symbol designed by Master Svietliy
Formatted by Jennifer Woodhead, Gaia Design Studio
Edited by Dan Taggart
Featured Artist, Chiara Mecozzi

DEDICATION

For All Wild Women

TOGETHER WE BLOOM

CONTENTS

PREFACE

This book was a labor of love and represents a decade of deep, personal, internal work. It took nine months to write and ten years to gain the experience necessary to write it. I really do believe that there comes a point when we need to do more than read other people's stories. We need to write our own. If reading is the inhale, writing is the exhale and both are required to live.

In 2010 I knew that someday I would write something worth reading. I wrote my first book in 2015 and scrapped it. I began again in 2017 and scrapped it. In 2018 I was halfway through a third, and for a third time, I deleted the entire document. It wasn't what I was supposed to bring into the world. I believe that books are already written before the author ever starts. Books choose their author long before the author knows what to write. This book prepared me, refined me, and nurtured me for a long time before it allowed me to write it. Authors are simply vessels in need of fine-tuning before they can become a channel to bring what is needed into the world. This book took 10 years to write because before it could be opened, I had to open. For 9 years and 3 months, I broke open one small crack at a time. The more I opened, the more acquainted I became with the voice that had been waiting to speak through me. The more I opened, the more access I gained to a power greater than I'd ever known.

For nine months I wrote without knowing what I was really doing. It wasn't until the day I finished this book that I realized what it had become. This book teaches you how to open. It is a guide back to the truest version of yourself. It will lead you down a path that opens you to the higher power within so that you too can become a vessel of love, light, and truth for this world.

The world needs you, *all* of you. It is my greatest desire that these pages will inspire you to step into your power and fully embrace the feminine life-force you have always been; that you choose a life of freedom and remember what it means to be Wild.

SAFE HARBOUR

INTRODUCTION

I am interested in women who want more from this life. I am looking for women who drip with passion, who move boldly, and who crave depth. These are the women I am speaking to because they are the women who turn the world. They are the women who lead us back to the Heart.

If you are reading this, you are one of these women. Like me, you are the women who have been told you are too much, too big, too loud, too fast, too loose, too sexual, and too Wild. Perhaps you are one of these women who wants to change the world, but struggles to know what to do or how to step into your feminine power so that you can live the life of freedom and purpose you yearn for.

We struggle because we have been so culturally and sexually repressed, we don't even realize it anymore. We can no longer feel how deep the suppression and oppression runs. This social and cultural conditioning is so much a part of our environment, we are like fish in a bowl, and the hardest thing to be aware of is the water we are swimming in.

Because of this social/cultural suppression, we are prevented from realizing our full potential as women. We need to remove the shackles of cultural conditioning and give ourselves permission to embrace our full feminine power. We need to return to being Wild.

The Wild is your soul's home. It is your natural state of free, unbridled expression. It is where all creativity is born, where all passion is enjoyed, and where all love is given and received. It is erotic, beautiful, and empowering. It is divine, and it is feminine.

The word *Wild* has nothing to do with what we might define as crazy, deranged, mad, fanatical, or a loss of control. Rather, it is a surrender to and acceptance of our most natural state, a state stripped free of repressive social constructs, limiting conditioning, and false beliefs about what it means to be a woman. When you fully embody your Wild nature and embrace your natural, untamed feminine sexuality, you unleash the woman you are meant to be. Returning to our Wild feminine nature does not mean going crazy. What *is* crazy is fearing what we really desire and ignoring who we really are.

You innately possess divine and unlimited power. As a woman, it is essential that you proudly own that power and reclaim your natural femininity. It is time to let yourself be seen, heard, and felt. Your power is always present within you, but it is up to you to give it full expression in your life.

From childhood, male-dominated culture conditioned us to hide, to cover, and to shrink the very parts of ourselves that give us our power and the world its life.

"Don't dress like that. They'll think you're a slut."

"Cross your legs. Be lady-like."

"Speak softly. Women shouldn't be so loud."

"Don't make the first move. Men won't respect you."

And above all... "Don't enjoy sex too much. It makes you dirty, bad, and gross."

Little by little, and in a dangerously subtle way, we are taught to be less than who we really are.

Let this be an urgent invitation to reclaim the parts of you that have been stifled, blocked, cut short, limited, ignored, shunned, choked, hidden, feared, and suppressed in any way. Let it all rise back to the surface now. It is safe to welcome back the parts of your Wild self that were lost to culture, tamed for religion, buried in schooling, hidden from family, and submitted to an unenlightened world.

Do not listen
To the ones who say you burn too big,
too bright, too hot.
Do not listen
To the ones who say you show too much,
feel too deep, speak too loud.
Do not listen
To the ones who say, "this is what a woman should be
— and you are not that!"
The truth is, these are the ones who can not handle your heat.
They cannot handle your truth. They cannot handle your love.
They are the ones who have boxed you into a false reality that
cannot grow, that cannot change, that cannot allow you to
open, expand, and break free.
Do not listen. They have no business here.
Their limitations were never yours to carry.
Of course you are too much for the ones who are not willing to
be everything they are.
So, Be Too Much.
Burn, flood, storm, and quake.
Because you are made of Woman.
You, WOMBan, are Everything.
I know this doesn't scare you.
It doesn't scare you because you know— it sets you free.

—Indigo

I wrote this book for the woman who yearns for freedom from all limitations. I wrote this for the woman who wants to change the world- Her world. Ultimately, I wrote this book for myself. I wrote it to help myself remember who I really am, to give myself permission to be all that I am, and to encourage myself to fully embody my divine feminine nature by reclaiming my Wild power.

While writing this book, I have shed layers of false beliefs and limiting conditioning, resurrected dead and buried parts of myself, returned to my most natural state, and have become the woman I want to be. I have changed the world because I have changed *my* world.

Returning to the Wild is a rebellious act. It is a conscious choice to live differently than most of the world. I can promise you that there is freedom to be found in that choice. My hope is that this book will give you the courage to reclaim your feminine power, and save you the time and pain from having to travel this path alone, without guidance or support.

We are in this together.

It is safe to set yourself free.

It is safe to be Wild.

FOR ME, FOR MY DESIRE, FOR MY LOVE

*Woman is the original rebel, the first revolutionary, the real Wild,
and the birthplace of all creation. She is not the fall from innocence
but the rise from ignorance. She is not the fall from paradise, but the
rise to enlightenment.*

– Indigo

CUT FROM OUR ROOTS

I t is disturbing that we no longer recognize our natural selves. We are so disconnected from feeling; the Earth, each other, our bodies, our cycles, our sexuality, and ourselves, that we miss the very abundance of sensual life we were born to create and enjoy.

This disconnection happens because we have replaced our holistic feminine feeling with linear masculine thinking as a result of ubiquitous, patriarchal cultural conditioning, the shaming of sex, and millennia of feminine suppression. We are afraid to feel and claim our own power because we have been taught that it is either dangerous or evil. We are afraid to feel and accept our own Wild nature because we have been fooled into adopting shame-based beliefs that if a woman does not appear, think, and behave in certain ways she must be crazy, manipulative, bitchy, bossy, broken, or damaged. Instead of risking this perception, we settle for domesticated, shallow, and less than remarkable lives.

To accept a cultural, religious, social, or traditional definition of what a woman is or what is acceptable for her to do, be, and have, contradicts your spirit. It negates your feminine being.

Woman, Be

Will you choose to rise above identity?
Connect to inner spirituality
Expand and create your own reality
By embracing your sovereign sexuality

Woman, Be

Will you transcend this prison of duality?
Proudly step into divine totality
Choose to embody this feminine vitality
And sink into your natural sensuality

Woman, Be

You were made to run wild and free
To outshine illusion and insanity
With your love unite all of Humanity
Answer the call, and you will soon see-
Woman, you are here to simply Be.

- Indigo

FOR US, FOR ALL, FOR LOVE

I am willing to bet that you were never taught how to really feel, accept, and process your pain and that a disconnection from your feminine nature and sexuality has become a major source of this pain.

I am willing to bet that you were never encouraged to lean into your Wild essence and embrace your natural joy.

I am also willing to bet you have never allowed your feminine nature and sexuality to be the source of that joy.

We have been born into a culture that is cut from the root of feminine being and we are not taught how to re-root ourselves. The injury of being cut off from your greatest internal gift and power bleeds over into your external world, manifesting as co-dependent relationships, the inability to fully pursue passions, and an overarching theme of blocked, limited, stifled living.

The disconnection from your Wild, your natural state as a woman, and the knowledge of the true source of your power keeps you trapped and small. It keeps you in a place hopelessly and desperately grasping for the freedom and fulfillment you desire. This happens because rather than being shown that your freedom, sovereignty, and power comes from your own natural feminine roots, you have been taught to deny this and seek it elsewhere. Thus, you have placed all power and faith in people, places, and things outside of yourself. We all understand that a branch of a tree does not grow by dipping its leaves into a bowl of water every now and then. It lives and thrives from water brought up by its roots from the Earth. We are no different. Disconnection from our Wild, earthy roots leads to a shriveled, unfulfilling existence.

The greatest emotional trauma we can experience is disconnection from our roots, which represent our natural selves. Disconnection breeds indifference, stifles joy, and keeps you chained to a reality bearing the rules and limitations of those who would have you live quiet and tamed in a little cultural cage.

You will not live the life you want to live if you do not learn to reconnect to your most real and natural self by sinking your roots deeply back into your Wild femininity; your true nature. To do this you must be willing to abandon the false beliefs surrounding women, femininity, sex, sexuality, and sensual expression that have been embedded in our culture for millennia.

"Finding yourself" is not really how it works. You aren't a ten-dollar bill in last winter's coat pocket. You are also not lost. Your true self is right there, buried under cultural conditioning, other people's opinions, and inaccurate conclusions you drew as a kid that became your beliefs about who you are. "Finding yourself" is actually returning to yourself. An unlearning, an excavation, a remembering who you were before the world got its hands on you."

—Emily McDowell

I promise this book will teach you simple, immediate ways to cultivate your feminine presence and re-root into the source of your true Wild power. As you do so, you will also establish a deeper, more meaningful connection to everything around you, the Earth, a higher power, and to the people you love most. You will find that it is all part of you. This book will help you shed layers of fear, doubt, false and limiting beliefs, and the cultural conditioning that has kept you from true independence. This book will wake you up to your feminine power and to **the Wild Woman you already are** so that you can start living the life you were meant to live and find the joy and fulfillment you desire and deserve.

THE CALL OF THE WILD

There is a difference between the things that beckon us and the things that call from our souls. We are beckoned by outer energies, that steal and drain our time and attention. A call from the soul is infinite; it is timeless, and comes from within. It is the Wild calling out to you urging, "Come here. This is the way."

If you have found yourself feeling stuck in a day-to-day routine that seems to bury your spirit alive, you have felt the call.

If you have ached to experience a life beyond the stifling rules of a domesticated society, you have felt the call.

If you feel hopelessly trapped in a sensual deadzone your heart does not recognize, you have felt the call.

If you have yearned for freedom, independence, and a life full of uninhibited passion, you have felt the call.

We all feel it eventually, and the longer we wait to answer, the more painfully we feel its pull.

What we often experience as an irresistible craving for something more, is the call of the Wild. It is the call of your soul begging you to wake up and come home.

The Wild is your soul's true home. It is found in reclaiming, exploring, and embracing your feminine sexuality by freeing it from generational cycles of shame and deprivation. It is found in repairing the connection to your body and by honoring the deep longing you have to intimately connect with others, and with the Earth.

Without awakening and honoring their innate wildness, and without learning to rewrite old stories that have buried feminine nature and sexuality in thick layers of fear and shame, I have seen women cut off from their creativity, enslaved at jobs they despise, and weighed down by heavy burdens they were never meant to bear. When the Wild is embraced, balanced, and integrated it wages an internal revolution that brings about external liberation.

The Wild Woman within is as awake as you are aware. She is as powerful as you are present. Without her we forget why we are here; **to realize our divinity and uplift humanity.**

Reading the words "Wild Woman" elicits an arousing response within all of us. We feel something stir deep inside, reminding us that we desire something more than a life caged and controlled by screens. Far too often, our feminine intuition is drowned out by to-do lists, schedules, money problems, and worries about what other people think about how we choose to live our lives. The list of soul-deadening distractions goes on and on. Once we re-root into our Wild nature, we are able to let go of these small concerns and nourish what is most important for our souls. We are able to honor our hearts, pursue what we really love, and fulfill what we are meant to do in the world.

The call of the Wild is answered when you fully embody and express your Wild femininity. Write your story, speak your truth, dance your feelings, paint your thoughts, dress artfully, pursue your passions vigorously and open your heart to this world. You will never have this chance again.

"There is a vitality, a life force, an energy, a quickening that is translated through you into action, and because there is only one of you in all time, this expression is unique. And if you block it, it will never exist through any other medium and will be lost."

- Martha Graham

Returning to your Wild means connecting with yourself in deeper ways than our repressive culture allows, and awakening the primal and Wild parts of your soul that have been hidden or tamed for social acceptance. This is not a road traveled by the faint of heart. It is the road traveled by women who desire truth and independence.

This is the path to feminine awakening, empowerment, and freedom.

GAIA

The soul has a need for Wild.

WAKING UP YOUR WILD WOMAN

"Within every woman there is a wild and natural force, filled with good instincts, passionate creativity, and ageless knowing. Her name is: Wild Woman. But she is an endangered species." -

- Clarissa Pinkola Estes

Women live remarkable lives when they know who they are. When we are willing to accept every part of ourselves and embrace each aspect in a shameless and unapologetic way, we come to real self-knowledge grants access to true self-love. We all want to live remarkable lives. We all want to fully and unapologetically love ourselves. So why don't we feel like we do? I believe it is because we have split ourselves in two. There is the "nice girl" we pretend to be and the Wild Woman we really are inside. Fortunately, this gap can be mended. By remembering and honoring your true desires, by embracing your Wild nature, and by exploring your feminine sexuality, you awaken and set free the Wild Woman within.

My hope is that this book will make you feel safe and supported in remembering who you really are, and in pursuing who you really want to be. We live in a world that demands uniqueness and originality (especially from women), but praises and rewards the status quo (especially in women). I want to help you reject these mixed messages and discover your personal power. I want to help you gently remove every piece of culturally conditioned nonsense so that you can see and feel the beauty that is buried underneath.

As women, most of us (if not all), have become who we *were taught* to be, not who we really are. We learned to edit ourselves. Woefully, we routinely edit out our Wild disposition and intuitive flow, the very aspect of ourselves that frees our divine being. The idea of a "wild woman" or the Wild Woman archetype, elicits a sense of darker intensity, and even fear. She is undefinable, and so she is feared. She is feared, and so she is suppressed. The truth is, the more you suppress or deny her, the more stunted and crippled you become. Denial of the Wild leads to weakness and destruction. These destructive patterns play out both in our personal and collective lives. They eat away our soul from the inside- out.

To be Wild is not to be crazy or psychotic. It is not a loss of control, rather, it is the willingness to embody the things we are not meant to suppress. Our Wildness is what connects us to both our femininity and our divinity. It is found in our innate love for nature, our natural delight in pleasure, our longing to move freely, and our unquenchable curiosity for the unknown. The women who have changed the world share many things in common; tenacity, purpose, vision, confidence, and authenticity.

They are fearless and unashamed but most importantly, they reject social and cultural limitations.

Eve, Lilith, Hatshepsut, Cleopatra, Joan of Arc, Rosa Parks, Susan B. Anthony, Marie Curie, Amelia Earhart, Elizabeth Fry, Harriet Tubman, Sojourner Truth, Sarah Breedlove, Junko Tabei, Julia Butterfly Hill, Maya Angelou, Margaret Fuller, Waangari Maathai, Gloria Steinem, Malala Yousafzai, Greta Thunberg, and on, and on, and on.

We have all been touched by some model or version of the Wild Woman. She is the woman who is an unstoppable force of passion, boldness, and creativity, the woman who moves and inspires us through full feminine embodiment. Whether or not you have recognized this, the Wild Woman lives in and through women you meet every day. We meet her each time a woman sets new standards of living by freeing herself from shame, surrendering to her true nature, rejecting the status quo, overcoming oppressive cultural boundaries, and transcending all limitations.

The Wild Woman fits no single mold.

She is the woman who unravels old stories and writes her own.

She is the woman who explores and embraces her sexuality.

She is the woman who defies rules set by others to control and limit her joy and power.

She is the woman who deeply connects with her origin, her nature, and her truth.

She is the woman who rejects definition and lives in alignment with her heart's desire, no matter how much her path may conflict with cultural norms and taboos.

The Wild Woman is unafraid to reject society's rules and norms in order to make the changes she knows are important and necessary for her freedom and progression. You know her by the way her feminine presence impacts your own life and consciousness. You know her by the way she seems to compel you in the direction of your own soul's longing. You know her because her Wildness awakens and stirs your own. You know her because she is *you*.

This is your wake up call.

"No matter by which culture a woman is influenced,
she understands the words wild and woman,
intuitively."

– Clarissa Pinkola Estés

FEMININE NATURE

SHINE

WILD (ADJ.)

1. Untamed, unrestricted, uninhibited, free. 2. Pristine, untarnished, unspoiled, pure. 3. As nature intended, authentic, genuine, real, true to itself.

NATURE (N.)

1. The fundamental qualities or characteristics that together define the identity of something. 2. The inherent, inborn features of a person, place, or thing. 3. A creative, controlling force in the universe.

I found this section difficult to write. I am required to use words, which move to define and describe something that cannot fit a single definition. I got in my own way when I'd sit down to think about how to define the characteristics that make up our nature as women. I was stuck here for days before I realized that my struggle was actually showing me what my Wild feminine nature requires. Amidst this struggle, I was reminded that if I am to connect to my feminine nature, I am required to be in a place of feeling, not thinking. Femininity is a quality of curves and flexibility, not straight lines and rigid forms.

Our nature runs deeper than learned behaviors, acquired traits, or developed qualities. When we speak of our feminine nature, we are speaking of those aspects that are innate, embedded, untamed, pristine, and pure. They are coded into your DNA and woven into your being.

My only goal in this section is to help you *feel* into your undefined, innate, and Wild self. Rather than tell you what your nature is or isn't, I'd like to invite you to finish the statement, "it is my nature to _____." I did this over and over again until I felt full. I will share my list below;

It is my nature to wander and explore.

It is in my nature to evolve and expand.

It is my nature to change my mind when I learn or feel something new.

It is my nature to need time alone.

It is my nature to care for plants and animals

It is my nature to connect with the ocean and the moon.

It is my nature to feel alive in my own body.

It is my nature to be sexy and sexual.

It is in my nature to experience things sensually.

It is my nature to create beautiful spaces.

It is my nature to feel things deeply.

It is my nature to know exactly what to do next, even if it makes no logical sense.

It is my nature to share myself with the world and to allow myself to be seen and heard.

It is my nature to dance, sing, and play.

It is my nature to rest and relax.

It is my nature to love and be loved.

It is my nature to...

As you write, notice if any of your daily behaviors contradict what you know and feel to be your true nature. This is how you can start to identify the layers of conditioning that keep you from expressing your femininity in a full, authentic, and unique way. If you have a difficult time identifying aspects of your feminine nature or connecting with yourself in this way, my advice is to lead with desire. We are able to reconnect with and express our true nature through our desires. For example, I have the desire to eat intuitively because it is my nature to feel alive in my own body. It is in my nature to listen to my own inner authority. Maybe your desire is to become a poet or a performer. It may be in your nature to express and move your unique perspective of life and love. Life is love in motion. It is artistic and creative. Allow your desire to move through you. Make love to your life. Desire, when true and authentic, is a powerful tool because it leads you back to your most natural self. It is not something to attach to, rather, it is something to follow.

Yarixa's Story

Unleash Me

Unleash me.
I'm ready to be free.
Dance with me.
It's An invitation to connect and be.
My heart is wide open.
The poetry is being spoken.
I'm ready for your untamed love.
You wild thang.
Such a white lion dove.
Ravage me. Take me.
Penetrate me with your wildness.
Kill me with your kindness.
Feel this electricity. You make me cum in your lucidity.
Unlock my creativity.
I'll reflect your divinity.
Shatter my shackles.
I love your rebellious radical.
This love Is boundless. It's timeless.
Unleash me.

And you will simultaneously be free.
I release you from any and all responsibility.
Any pain I might feel, I will allow so I can heal.
I will rage like an animal in a cage.
I will cry like a newborn babe.
I will dance like a dragon,
Spit fire the color of the radio flyer wagon
I'll transmute through the moans of my orgasms
As you sing me songs from your record albums
Like chocolate I'll melt in the heat
Lick me , now I'm even more enjoyably sweet
These chains no longer have a grip.
They dissolve as I let my tears drip.
Stay with me. Look at me.
You won't die in your vulnerability.
I'm here to show you love unconditionally.
Kiss me like you know how...
surrender to this love now.
As you unleash me, I unleash you
I am the truth you already knew

-Yarixa Ferrao

Let's Unleash together.

I have so many stories to tell you about the path to Unleashing myself wildly, I could write an entire book about it. But, for now, I'll tell you one of my favorites.

Burning Man 2017

(panting) "What the Fuck?" ....WHAT the fuck?.... What the fuck?!" I said three times while panting, out of breath and in shock, while looking at this 6'5" strong black, almost naked (a rope around his waist and a cloth covering his parts), heavenly earthly creature of a man right in front of me who's name was Wusu. A King in his own right; one of the most captivating men I had ever met. We had both ended up on our knees on the playa dust floor at my first Burning Man, after fiercely dancing together the dance of our life! In that moment he gripped my hand tightly, gave me a hug, looked at me while laughing with a face of being in shock too and responded with the same phrase "What the fuck?!"

I then looked up and out and saw an entire crowd of people spectating in a formulation of a circle around us, in which some were clapping, some cheering and others just staring at us with jaws dropped.

I looked to the side, and my friend Hart comes in closer, grabs whatever part of my body she could, and with her bright blue eyes wide open and her mouth in awe says

"What the fuck Yari?… Okay, You and Wusu HAVE to be in my music video and you HAVE to do this for work!"

I looked at her with the same surprised face that almost everyone had and said " I know! But, I don't know how? But yes, I know! Shit!"

You see, dancing was one of my BIGGEST fears! Up until that year at the age of 35, I had never truly danced the way my soul wanted to. I was scared to look weird, to not do the dance moves right, to look too sexy, too sexual or too slutty. Ultimately I was scared of being judged and made fun of because all I wanted was to fit in, be liked and loved.

I had traumatic experiences as a kid being bullied and not being accepted for who I was. Thereafter I suffered greatly in love and relationships due to a low self esteem and not knowing really who I was.

Sex and my body became the basis of my relationships and became my self worth. I got married to a man because he checked basically everything off my 'list', loved me without sex being a priority, yet I deceived myself by not taking into account my real life experience and how I was actually feeling with him. At the time, I was doing the best I could, but I wasn't allowing my full authenticity to shine through. I thought to myself that if I let out what really wanted to come out, there was a high possibility of my marriage failing, not fitting into my family's or society's standards and being pushed away and rejected. And, I stuffed it down and kept going about life. Except my soul wasn't having it and my body fiercely responded.

I had a stomach ache almost everyday, I didn't have sex drive for 6 years, I developed a cyst adjacent to my ovary that created pain every time I had sex and I became depressed from the onset of marriage. I got to a point I couldn't eat anything at all except for juicing and even that made me nauseous. I became so tired I had to take sleep in between clients. My life became routine and boring AF.

Somewhere in the middle of all that, at around the age of 30, I remember saying to myself, "In my next lifetime, I'm going to be a dancer." as if there was no chance in the world it could possibly happen in this one.

I would watch TV shows like *So You Think You Can Dance* and sometimes cry or cheer on the dancers because it was so beautiful and activating to my soul. I would see how free and expressed they were and would light me up. At the same time, they would make me wanna hide my expression even more.

I was resisting dying, trying to hold on to the false layers of identity that I adopted since I was a child.

After a long time of suffering and unexpressed pain, I had to let myself die. What I am referring to is the me that was playing out the inauthenticities. Can you relate?

I finally ended up getting a divorce and leaving behind the parts of me that were deceptive. It was like cleaning out my closet and getting rid of the shit that I no longer wore.

This was a huge turning point and life for me began again. No more stomach aches, got my libido back, my energy came back and I became excited again. This time I was going to create my life EXACTLY as wild, playful and as full-on unicorn magical as I could dream it to be.

I dreamt of being surrounded by artists, musicians, open minded entrepreneurs here to change the world. I dreamt of exploring my sexuality with both men and women and becoming free of the traditional form of relationship I was taught. And I dreamt of myself becoming an artist, a creative, a dancer and musician in my unique way. I wrote all this down in my journal, in present tense one morning after about 2 months of being divorced and within a week's time the synchronicities started taking place in real time.

Imagine what I was feeling when I looked at Wusu, the crowd of people and my friend Hart, whom all had just validated to me I was a dancer- in *this* time life. Not only that but, I was hearing I was intended to bring dance into my work. What?! How?

Life was presenting me again with a choice; I was to either take this opportunity that made my spirit sing more than anything else in the world and run with it or I was to allow all the thoughts like, "How am I gonna teach? I've never even taken one choreography class. How am I going to incorporate this into my work? What if I can't? What if I fail?" that would squash my soul's dreams and commit the same mistake as I had in the past that had led me to live a mundane 'safe' life, while dying painfully everyday.

Fuck that! I chose to LIVE and I ran with it!

Unleash! - a guided transformational dance journey and my most sacred work, was born.

As for the "How", it resolved itself. I just showed up. I asked God to show me and within a week it became clear that I was not here to teach dance, I was here to inspire through my dance and create a space to set others free.

Because I listened to my inner voice, thousands of people have been transforming their lives, joyfully expressing themselves in ways they never thought possible, and paying it forward by stepping into their power, sharing their gifts with the world.

The more I have followed my highest excitement and faced my fears the more I have stepped and keep stepping into my power.

The more I have gotten to love and accept the divine, warrior, Goddess, Shaman, Alchemist, fiery and grounded force of nature I am, the more pleasure filled, joyful, FUN AF, and magical my life is and the easier it is to give my gift.

Unleash! has allowed me to speak in front of hundreds of people (what was once my biggest fear), dance explicitly in the rawness of how spirit wanted to move through me while being completely naked and on my period without batting an eyelash, more of my artistry to come alive, meet the most magical and creative people on the face of the planet that have continued the fuel of inspiration, be creative at all times, be interviewed in popular podcasts and other media outlets to broadcast my message larger and wider, share my story in this book, give a platform to artists and facilitators to share their gifts, answer the call of those asking for a place like this to exist and lastly, a space that allows me to be me and you to be you.

Almost EVERY SINGLE thing that I wrote down after my divorce is my life now.

Has this path been easy? No.

Has it been painful? Yes.

Has it been the most fulfilling thing in the entire world and worth every second? Infinitely, YES.

At the end of my life as Yarixa, I will have shed all of the deceptive masks and programming that had kept me and my ancestors from being fully free. I will have set the stage for a new world, where children are born in a place that all beings are at peace in their highest form of truth. I will have done my part and walk out 'fully empty'- given it my all, with nothing else left.

Here are a few main things I've learned along the way,

1. Fear is the mask that freedom wears.
2. With the embrace of individuality, you create unity in the world.
3. The more you are YOU, the more you get paid. Money stops becoming a thing out there and you become the curren(t)cy- the flow of the limitless abundance that is available to you, when you get out of your own way.
4. Dancing, singing, breathwork, movement, play and music are the keys to unlocking the gift, magic and beauty you are.

And here are a few words of advice:

1. Follow your highest excitement
2. Face your fears
3. Speak your truth
4. Forgive yourself
5. Do what you love without compromising
6. Journal, write it down.
7. Support and nourish your body so it can support you in all you are here to be and do.
8. When you don't know the answer, take a breath, ask Source, your angels and guides for assistance.
9. Turn your pain to beauty, opportunity and art!

With that last piece of advice, I wanted to leave you with this poem called, "I've come in the name of liberation."

The Rules and Regulations...
Bring me to a ranging sensation
Wearing these masks of suffocation
A maddening manifestation
Of a sense of separation
When all we want is freedom and unification
I've come in the name of liberation
Awakening from deceptive hallucination
I'll chew up fears
Digest with tears
And spit out crystals clear
I'll change weeds to flowers

I'll chant for hours
And turn pains into powers
I'm an alchemist, a catalyst, an activist
A passion provoker
I'll unleash your choker
I'm a sourceress
A dragoness
A butterflying metamorphosis
I'm a mystical miracle
Not your stereotypical
An in your face visual
Ain't nothin subliminal
Primal, instinctual
A wise intellectual
I see through the veils
I see what they're doing to the dolphins and the whales
I've come to breathe & exhale
Release the stories, programs & tales
Exposing the dark and depressing
By Jungleling wild and expressing
Living it up and trailblazing
I'm a shaman
Yess man
I enter into life's complexity
To bring forth simplicity
Wildly I'll dance
I'll take the chance

This life is free will
No regrets
I'll be at peace and die still
Giving it my all
I free fall
I'll tip the point
Smoke a joint
leave behind a radical legacy
That cuts through the jealousy,
blasts through supremacy,
and brings joy, play and prosperity
I'm led by inspiration
To lay a better foundation
For children of the future generations

I love you. Thank you, and Unleash that ish!

Yarixa Ferrao,
Creatrix of Unleash!
@COACHYARI
@UNLEASHMOVEMENT

Throughout this book, I will continue to share women's stories of transformation. I include these because I want you to understand that any transformation we experience is ultimately a step towards returning to the Wild. I want to show how powerfully diverse this can look. No matter how it takes place, what really happens each and every time is women learn to step into their power by following their desires and their dharmic path, it returns them to their most natural selves. Reclaiming your Wild Woman means following your path, answering the call of *your* heart and committing to the life *you* truly want to live, no matter what you were taught or what circumstances befell you.

Our stories, no matter where or how they're told, become models and metaphors for others. My hope is that you will find yourself in each of these women and their stories of transformation. My desire is that they will continue to inspire you to live fully and wildly so that one day you will write and share your own story with others. When we write and share our own stories, it creates a ripple effect. They spark an undeniable "me too" feeling and encourage other women to move deeper into their natural, untamed, and Wild selves.

As women, it is your nature to live and express from a place of heart and soul. It is our nature to be free to think, free to move, free to speak, free to behave, and free to feel. When we are told to think, move, speak, act, or be a certain way in order to be considered a "good woman", a "strong woman", or a "desirable woman", it not only negates our nature, it stifles our soul's growth.

No matter the forces in play that cause us to feel disconnected and under-expressed, it is not our job to fight them (as waves of popular feminism do). Our only job is to free ourselves from the obligation to abide by these false and limiting standards by expressing ourselves fully and authentically through living our individual truths and answering the call of our Wild souls. This is how we break the pattern of suppressed and shallow living. It can stop with us.

Though we evolve and expand, our nature is the part of us that stays true and consistent no matter what else changes in our lives or the world around us. Our nature includes the deeper aspects of ourselves that are always present but not always noticed. Things like our intuition, our cycles, our creative processes, and our need to express ourselves authentically. The more that you can connect with these parts of yourself and begin to consciously apply them each day, the easier it is to live in alignment with your soul's path that leads to a life of enjoyment and freedom.

ASPECTS OF FEMININE NATURE

Feeling & Intuition

It is your nature to experience and process life through feeling and emotion. This is why women seem to act on "hunches", gut-feeling, or intuition often without the mental justification of "logic" or "rationalization" to back it up. This is not our weakness, it is our genius. We often quickly recognize and identify when people, places, and things seem "off". We "feel it in our bones" when it is time to say something, say nothing, leave where we planned to spend the evening, or go somewhere we never planned to be at all.

I like to imagine my intuition as the part of me that is closest to my soul or higher self. It is the part of me that knows without being told, that understands without explanation, and that firmly leads as long as I am still enough to listen. She is the guide I can count on when I feel crippled by mental uncertainty.

Twice in the last 5 years, I have had strong, inexplicable feelings that it was time to quit my job. Each time I quit, it was a job that paid me well, gave me the flexibility to work from home, and were generally positive work environments. There was no obvious reason that I, or anyone for that matter, would want to quit. However, my internal compass pointed so strongly in another direction, it would have been painful to stay. Both times I felt this, I was terrified. I was terrified and did it anyway. Each time, what followed and opened up in my life was nothing short of miraculous. It was a very real way to learn and feel that there is something great inside of me at work, something I don't need to understand fully, in order to trust it totally. We are given feelings, nudges, directions, and information all the time. Our power is in our willingness to follow it without question, whether or not fear is present. Fear is in the mind and manifests as thought-loops of doubt and worry. Intuition is in the body. It speaks from the deep sensation within the center of your being. It is a place of feeling and true knowing.

"You will never follow your own inner voice until you clear up the doubts in your mind."

− Roy T. Bennett

"Intuition is a sense of knowing how to act spontaneously, without needing to know why... It means exactly what it sounds like, in-tuition! An inner tutor or teaching and learning mechanism that takes us forward daily. It is a resource that, when recognized, has infinite potential."

− Sylvia Clare

Though we are talking about women specifically, this is not to say that men do not have or experience similar things. They do. And when they do it is their own feminine energy at work. Physical gender has to do with our sexual reproductive organs, whereas, masculine and feminine energies (i.e. yin and yang) are two sides of the same coin that exist within all of us. As women, we are the physical expression of the feminine and thus, the feminine energy is generally more active within us and at work in our lives. While masculine energy expresses itself as ideation and direction, feminine energy seeks to express itself through creation, destruction and growth. It naturally seeks an environment of peace and harmony and avoids violence, pain, and conflict. Thus pleasure, love, and joy are an outgrowth of feminine energies within us. As women, this is the basis of our power.

Developing a strong connection with your intuition can be challenging, especially if you've spent a lifetime second-guessing yourself or not trusting your own feelings because of too many other "voices" in your head. These are voices of self-doubt, blame, and judgment that you have been handed down by our culture and they are drowning out your intuition. The voice of your intuition is only as loud as you allow it to be. The ways we connect with and develop our intuition to make wiser more soul-inspired decisions, are subtle and require our presence and attention.

Intuition is usually not loud or demanding. Most often, it is soft and can go completely unnoticed if we do not quiet our busy, thinking minds. We have to learn to recognize when and how intuition communicates within our bodies and our spirits or energetic systems. Direction from your intuition may come in physical sensations like goosebumps, pressure in your stomach, sharp pain in your head, or a quickening heartbeat. Intuitive messages may come dressed as emotions, such as sudden feelings of uneasiness or confusion to help steer you away from people or things that are not meant for you. You may also catch feelings of euphoria or profound peace when you are in the right place at the right time. As you become more familiar with the way your natural intuition speaks to you, you may even be able to begin a dialogue with this inner guide to uncover more information and gain more clarity. Ask yourself, "What am I listening to?" Notice if you are listening to the thoughts spinning in your mind or if you are able to listen to deeper sensation. Thoughts can mislead and misguide. Sensation never lies.

Pausing to create inner stillness is a powerful way to reconnect with your nature and remember how the deeper, constant parts of yourself work. Time set aside for listening is crucial. Our intuition cannot speak if thoughts are in overdrive. I like to light incense, make a comfortable place for myself on the floor, and sit until I feel a "shift". This is usually when insights or direction will begin to flow. It is how I wrote most of this book. A shift in energy indicates a shift in consciousness. It means we have opened ourselves to the unseen world. If we can choose to listen to the voice of our intuition over the constant chattering of our minds, we will be guided and directed down a path that leads to the life experiences we desire most.

Feeling is a form of listening. When you feel this inner voice, take immediate action. Intuition rewards your action and becomes stronger each time you respond. If we do not act on what we feel, we eventually lose the ability to feel at all. The more faith you place in your intuition, the greater the connection and guidance will be. Trusting your intuition is ultimately about trusting yourself, and the more trust you place in yourself, the more fulfillment you will have.

"When women reassert their relationship with the wildish nature, they are gifted with a permanent and internal watcher, a knower, a visionary, an oracle, an inspiratrice, an intuitive, a maker, a creator, an inventor, and a listener who guide, suggest, and urge vibrant life in the inner and outer world."

– Clarissa Pinkola Estes

CYCLES & SEASONS

As a woman, you were blessed with a body that is deeply connected to natural cycles, seasons, rotations, and patterns. Tuning into the flow of your physical body is essential to building a greater understanding of and connection to your natural self. Whether it is our menstruation cycle, our sleep cycle, our thirst and hunger cycle, the peaks and troughs of our physical energy, or the rise and fall of our sex drive, our body's cycles demonstrate an innate and unbreakable connection to the divine creation and destruction process.

When we tune into the flow of our bodies, our emotions, our thought patterns, and our day-to-day habits and routines, we open a window into the most real and Wild parts of ourselves. We see that there is a time to work and a time to play, a time to run and a time to rest, a time to laugh and a time to cry, a time to hold on and a time to let go, a time to give and a time to receive. The more aware we are of these cycles and how they sync with the Earth, with our desires, with our work, and with our relationships, the more power we have to begin working with and within these cycles and leveraging each phase and stage to our greatest benefit.

As women, it is a huge disservice to fight, resist, prolong, or cut short our natural flow. It is our nature to metaphorically live and die with these cycles and seasons. Most of us have a rather negative relationship with our moon cycle (period/ menstruation). This is the most uniquely feminine and natural cycle we experience, yet we attempt to turn it off any way we can. This is not to say that feminine hygiene products or birth control are bad and wrong, however, I would like to point out the emotional and psychological effect they have when they are used to block, dam, limit, and even completely stop our body's natural flow. We tend to associate our bleeding with feelings of dread and disgust. Because of this, we never learn what the phases of this cycle mean for our own experience and wellbeing.

Cree's Story

Once upon a time, I knew nothing about my cycle.

I was born into a world where menstruation was hardly talked about. It was so hush-hush and ridden with shame and this deep underlying tone of "there's something inherently wrong with being a woman."

When I first started bleeding, there was no welcoming into womanhood, honoring or celebration. I was never told that my blood is sacred. No one ever told me about the different hormonal fluctuations I would experience and how they influence the 4 different phases of my cycle.

I was never taught about any of these things by my mother. Neither was my mother, nor her mother's mother, nor many of the women in this modern westernized world.

What I did see was crazy PMS and painful periods. I grew up in a house with 6 women, all of them older than me.

This all just seemed normal. Nothing was ever talked about.

When I started bleeding I was distraught, I was super embarrassed and in tears, because I was with my dad and he had to take me to the store for pads! I called my mom and she talked to me briefly on the phone and said we would talk more once I was home. Once I got home, my mom and I talked. She told me I could use tampons or pads and taught how to use both. That's pretty much all I remember.

This is common among women. Many of them do not even tell their mothers, or anyone else for that matter, for years.

Throughout my teenage years growing up, I had very little concept of what it meant to have a deep, unyielding sense of self-love. I lived a lot of my life feeling very self-conscious and insecure. I was not comfortable in my body. I did not know how to embody my sacred flow. I had a faint, yet untapped sense of what it meant to embody the feminine and I certainly didn't have a sense of what solid sisterhood and positive female relationships were like. I had no idea what it actually meant to be an empowered woman.

When I was about 19, my world began to open up in a whole new way. I began to have an ever so subtle shift in my perspective around menstruation. It all started with a switch to organic tampons, without an applicator.

When I made the switch, something started to happen. I began to sense a connection to my body in ways that I hadn't before. I don't remember exactly how or when, but at some point, I started to get curious as to the deeper meaning of this whole period thing. Could it really be that women were just supposed to suffer through this time and live a life of embarrassment, shame, and hiding?

In 2011 I met a woman who changed the course of my life and opened my eyes to the sacredness of menstruation. My life has never been the same since. Over the course of the years to follow, I have been cultivating a relationship with my cycle in ways that up until that point I never knew were possible.

I started tracking my cycle and reading literature that spoke to something deep within me. I knew that there was something more to this menstruation thing, but hardly anyone I knew was talking about it!

For the first time ever, I began to discover that there was actually a pattern to my flow. I started to notice a certain level of predictability. I started feeling empowered and connected to a deep part of myself that seemed to be dormant, waiting for someone to wake her up. I started to establish a connection with my own inner sage, that part of me who holds all of the answers to questions I am seeking. I noticed that much of my cramping came from the fact that I wasn't listening to my womb, nor honoring the sacredness of my blood.

Discovering the power of my menstruation has been hands down, one of the single most powerful tools of empowerment and transformation in my life.

I have learned more about self-care and embodying my feminine nature by honoring my body and it's natural cycles than most other things.

The dance of learning to embody my flow is always ongoing. While there is a theme and a pattern, every cycle continues to be different, always mirroring back to me where I'm at in my life and what my general state of health and fertility is. Menstruation is like a monthly health report card.

I'm in tune with my inner sage.I'm more deeply connected to my intuition. I know when to rest, when to let go, when to be active and take action. I literally base my life around my cycle every single month and I've never felt more empowered. I know when to say yes, when to say no and when I need the most nurturance and care.

Cultivating a relationship with my cycle has bled over into every other aspect of my life. I had a previous partner say to me, "the way you are with your cycle and menstruation is different than the majority of the women I know in my life!"

This way of life is not new. Rather, I feel like I am tapping into an ancient way of a wisdom that was once contained by both men and women. Part of my mission is to bring about the revival of the Red Tent in this modern day.

Women need sacred spaces where they can be and bleed. Whether it be in their home or in their community. We need to reclaim the sacredness of this time and restore it to its rightful place.

The more that I have come into right relationship with

my cycle, the more everything in my life has come into right relationship.

I want you to know that you don't have to suffer through painful periods for all of your bleeding days. There's no need to feel ashamed, embarrassed, or cursed as a woman.

When a woman begins her first cycle, this is called menarche. This is her introduction to her power. Every time she bleeds, she gets to dance with her power. Once she crosses the threshold into menopause, she's living fully within her power.

Our society does not teach us this and it is my mission to help women to rediscover their power through honoring the sacred wisdom of menstruation. The time is now, we are the ones we have been waiting for.

Your cycle is not your enemy, it is your greatest ally. With this truth and knowledge restored in my own being, it is my greatest love and joy to teach other women how to honor their blood and come into right relationship with the power of their cycles.

Dear Sweet Wild Woman, I want to remind you of something that you may have forgotten. There is a wisdom that lies within your womb, the center of your being. The place that all life is birthed forth from whether literal or metaphorical. You may have forgotten this, at no fault of your own. You had no women before you to teach you, nor mentor you in the realms of the wild and mysterious terrain that is your menstrual cycle.

In fact, what you were taught was quite the opposite of this. Your blood is dirty, gross and something to be ashamed of. You are meant to quietly suffer, keep things hush-hush, never talking about it and most certainly never to men.

You were taught that the pain and suffering that many women experience with their blood and their cycle is simply 'part of being a woman'. It has become accepted as the norm, passed down from generation to generation, but sister, let me tell you a little secret. While this pain is common and seen as normal, it is not natural.

These are signs of our bodies crying out to us, our wombs reaching to get our attention in any way possible. They are relentlessly screaming out, but who is actually listening?

We were not made to suffer as women and our menstrual cycle is not part of a flawed design.

I will boldly say that your menstrual cycle has a very intelligent and genius design and is one of the most beautiful tools that I have ever discovered to help me navigate my life. It is your internal compass, your north star, guiding you home into the seat of your own soul.

It has the power to transport you into union with the divine, fill you with the nectar of sweet renewal, and download you with insight and inspiration in how to live a more aligned life. It will support you in releasing what is no longer serving so you have space to be filled with what is.

Your menstrual cycle serves as a monthly health report card, letting you know where there is imbalance and potential underlying health issues to be concerned about. She is warning you in advance. Not only on the physical level, but on an emotional, spiritual, and energetic level as well.

We are all experiencing the collective pain body of the feminine of years and lifetimes of neglect and disrespect. Our wombs and bodies are exhausted as they try to keep up with the buzz of modern-day life that goes against our inherently cyclical nature as women.

We keep fighting, pushing, and overriding this and her messages keep getting louder and stronger. When will we stop? When will we listen? When will we treat her with the deep respect and honoring that she deserves?

That's all she wants. She wants to be put into her rightful place and it's up to each and every one of us to do that.

For thousands of years, we have been denying ourselves of the cycle that makes life possible. It is because women bleed that every single one of us is born into this world. The menstrual cycle is the life cycle. Not only because it is the process that creates life, but it is the process that teaches us about the nature of life.

Women's bodies are a microcosm of the macrocosm. Our bodies mirror the body of the earth. Just like the earth's seasons ebb and flow through winter, spring, summer, and fall, so to do we through our inner seasons.

Our menstrual cycle not only mirrors the seasons of the earth, but it also mirrors the phases of the moon. As sister luna waxes and wanes from the new moon, to the full moon and back again, so to do we. The moon's average cycle is approximately 29 days, just like our menstrual cycle.

Over the years I have learned to come into right relationship with my own unique rhythm and flow as I've discovered the sacredness of my cycle, the sacredness of my blood and learned to embody my flow. There is nothing dirty, gross, or shameful about it. In fact, it is a beautiful and intelligent design serving as an initiatory journey into one's own wild power.

There is a Native American proverb that says, "At her first bleeding a woman meets her power. During her bleeding years she practices it. At menopause she becomes it."

Where are the wise women, where are our elders, aunties, and mothers who should be teaching us this wisdom from the time that we are young?

Although this wisdom has been lost, it has not been forgotten for it is ingrained deep into the cellular makeup of your being. It is ingrained in the memory of your bones and woven into your DNA. Can you feel it? It is longing to be awakened within. Your wild power lies dormant in your being. Are you listening?

It is longing to be awakened within you. It wants nothing more than to be remembered. Not only does she want to be remembered, but she is here to serve as your internal compass, guiding you home into the truth of who you are.

Oh sweet wild woman, may this evoke a stirring deep within you, something that you can no longer ignore. To do so is to deny yourself from experiencing the fullness of life as a woman who bleeds.

May this serve as an invitation, a beck and call to memories held deep within, may you begin to awaken as you reclaim the power of your period, the sacredness of your blood and step into your rightful place as a wild, dynamic, cyclical woman.

Cree Cox

Spiritual Guide & Menstrual Maven

WWW.CREECOX.COM

I encourage you to consciously shift your relationship with your feminine cycle into one of tenderness, love, and empowerment. Own all that you are. Welcome and connect with each part of your cycle. Learn to create with the natural flow of your body.

SENSUAL EXPRESSION

"The mystery of a woman lies in her sensuality."

— Lebo Grand

By nature, women are sensual beings. Sensuality brings your sexuality to life through the physical senses. Sexuality can exist without sensuality, but why would we want that? Sexuality without sensuality is nothing more than the automatic physiological responses of our bodies. Sensuality is a way of life, not just a sexual preference or style. It is full presence and living from your five common senses as well as your unlimited more subtle senses. A sensual life is a slower life, a life that pauses to take things all the way in. It is the exploration and gratification of smell, touch, taste, sight, sound, and every other finer feeling within the body. As women, if we want to live full, remarkable lives, we must learn to both experience and express life sensually.

Expressing ourselves sensually returns us to our Wild state. It is our sensuality that roots us back into our primal nature. This is because it connects the feedback our brain receives through our five primary senses, to our fundamental needs and desires. The more we can explore and expand ourselves in a sensual way, the more life we will truly live.

Our sensuality is enjoyed and expressed fully when we are committed to our own enjoyment. It is a choice to live sensually in every aspect of our lives. By grounding into our bodies, we come into full awareness. How full the moment is when we are slow enough to notice the brush of wind against our face, the pressure of our feet on the earth, the smell of blooming flowers, and the sunlight on our own skin. There is so much pleasure to be felt and experienced, even in the mundane, when we connect with our sensual, feeling body. It is our nature to feel it all.

"When we exercise our senses, feeling into the world as we move through it, smelling, tasting, touching, hearing, we awaken the wild inside us."

— Julie McIntyre

By fully embodying your Wild feminine nature, you simultaneously express earthly desire and divine being. Your wildness is your holiness. Some mistakenly believe that being Wild is somehow bad, wrong, or even something evil that must be shamed and tamed. This is not true. In fact, your Wild nature is the very definition of sacred. It is holy because it is wholly you. You can only be happy to the degree that you are whole. Your perfection is in your wholeness and wholeness includes all aspects of your nature and being. We have defined perfection in a way that excludes and limits certain things when really, true perfection is the allowance for all things. A woman who denies or suppresses any aspect of her Wild nature is by definition, not whole, and instead, crippled, stunted, or deformed. On the other hand, those women who fully embrace their Wild nature in all of its limitless, creative, sensual expression become whole; they are perfect.

Jeni's Story

We live in a culture with so much sexual shame. It's not talked about enough between women, between mothers and daughters, between sisters, or even between friends. My sexual reality came from verbal communication of what *not* to do and the most powerful communication; the silent energetic response of the nervous system.

I grew up in a strict religious home where covering up my body was a righteous wholesome act.

I never wore tank tops, sleeveless shirts, or bikinis. One-piece swimsuits only and shorts and dresses had to be down to at least the knees.

I was taught that girls who wore short shorts, tank tops and bikinis were sluts, had low self-esteem, had no respect for their bodies. They were just looking for attention and would definitely attract the wrong kind of people and experiences.

I didn't want to be one of those girls and I didn't want my girls to be one of those girls either. I truly believed that for years and lived by it faithfully. When I became a parent myself, I strictly taught my girls the same and shamed them for wanting to wear anything different.

I was curious about my body at a very young age. I remember being five and sitting in the tub and feeling the hot water against my vagina as I opened and closed my legs. The hot water rushing up against my genitals sending pleasurable tingling sensations into my vulva.

I remember hearing things like;

"Cover yourself up!"

"Don't run around naked, someone will see you!"

I remember feeling things like;

"Being naked is bad and unsafe."

"Someone might see your naked body and then want to touch your naked body. And that's bad."

I was so uncomfortable with my sexuality and nakedness that I completely shut down the natural part of my humanness.

The truth is, we are born from sex. There is not a human alive that has not come through the creation of sex and the portal of a woman's body. I feel like we have dehumanized a part of ourselves and others when we shame sex and our natural sexuality.

Babies will die without touch and yet as adults we still don't have approval for our own desires around touch and sex. I never received adequate sex education, let alone permission and approval to explore the natural humanness of my sex. To say my sexuality was shut down and locked up is an understatement.

In my world sex and marriage went together. Nothing else was possible or acceptable because this was set in stone by God. Outside of marriage, any type of sexual exploration and expression was a sin. The only thing that was acceptable was kissing.

As a child, I had a lot of sexual experiences. Most of those sexual experiences I liked. I felt so shameful liking being touched by an adult. It was called abuse and it was something shameful and bad, but I liked it. So, I must be really really bad.

My desire for sex was so intense it had to be covered up by pretending, so I didn't feel bad and others didn't think I was bad.

I felt like I was secretly seeking after this bad thing.

My desire for sex felt selfish and greedy.

As a teenager, I learned about the carnal sin of masturbation.

You do Not touch yourself. Ever!

As a teenager, I was reminded on a regular basis by my church leaders and parents about the sin and dangers of masturbation. Yes, I said dangers. I was taught masturbation was dangerous. Writing this now it sounds so ridiculous. What could be so dangerous right?

Masturbating at any age or time was a sin and dangerous.

Married, single, young or old, touching my vagina was a sin. I could become addicted if I masturbated. I would want to start watching porn. I would be tempted to have sex. I would be unsafe and I would do bad things. Once you were married your husband could touch you, but you couldn't touch yourself. And any sexual exploration of the same sex was unthinkable. Hell might be better and well suited for me if I had any thoughts about same-sex curiosity. So I didn't have any.

For a long time till in my late 30's, I was so ashamed and guilt-ridden I went to my clergyman to confess my sin. He told me my thoughts about the same sex were because of my childhood sexual abuse. It was okay to have them as long as I didn't act on them.

What the actual Fuck.

I have these sinful thoughts about women because I was sexually abused?!

My sense of what was natural, normal and what I had a choice of in sex was so backward. I had a lot of layers of shame and trauma around my sex. I was so ashamed about my desire for sexual pleasure I hid it inside like a secret. I thought if I was having sex then that was good sex.

Because not having it and wanting it was torturous, so just having sex was a relief from that.

Even when I was married, I felt so ashamed of my sexual desires. I was afraid of being seen as wanting it too much. I always wanted it more than my husbands and knew exactly how many days it had been since we had sex.

Because sex was bad and wrong outside of marriage if I wanted to have sex I had to get married.

I got married and divorced several times. When I was single I was always stretching that rule as far as my guilt would allow.

My sexual shame and guilt felt like a cork underwater. It was going to surface some time.

At 41 I was single and no longer a part of any religious group. I had left my religion but I wasn't free. I started to have sex and exploring, but I hid it from everyone that knew me.

I was so afraid of my power to choose sex outside of marriage I feared I would have sex with everyone. I would become the deepest shame that ran through me; a slut.

I wore my first bikini at 41. I literally felt like I was naked. I wore it around my house for a week before I had the courage to wear it out in public. It took me a few years to begin to unlock my sexuality and free myself from the prison of shame.

It started with me exploring what was a "yes" and what was a "no" during sex. I started having sex to just have the experience of having sex and not to have a relationship. I started a relationship with my pussy by looking at her in the mirror every day. I started to know and love all her folds and colors and see her as beautiful. Then, I started a practice of Orgasmic Meditation. I've spent a lot of time learning from my teachers about the personal responsibility that I have for my desire and for my sex. It's a power that doesn't sit lightly in my system.

I feel being responsible for my sexual power and desire is an essential part of what it means to be embodied in my feminine nature and energy.

My practice of Orgasmic Meditation continues to lead me down a path of deep connection with myself, my sexual expression, my body, and my sexual desires. Today at 47-years-old, my desire for sex and the type of sex I'm hungry for feeds my own sexual needs and my husband's.

- I am able to ask for what I want in sex and make connected adjustments.
- I am able to sit deeper in my body when receiving pleasure.
- I am able to hold the responsibility of my power with more awareness.
- I am able to feel deeply satiated and full in sex from an internal rightness in my being.
- I don't have great sex because my husband is such a great lover.
- I don't have great sex because my husband loves pussy and can't get enough of me.
- I have great sex because of me.
- I have great sex because of my relationship with myself.
- I have great sex because of my receptivity.
- I have great sex because of my ability to surrender and be open.
- I have great sex because of how connected I am to my body.

- I have great sex because of my willingness to use every past sexual experience (positive or negative isn't the point) as guiding direction to what I personally need to open and expand in my feminine sexuality.

When you cage your sexuality, you lock up a part of your soul regardless of what type of sexual relationship you are in.

My life's work has been to have access to *all* of me.

Access my power, access my sexuality, access my voice, and free myself from my own internal prison. When I do not have access to every aspect of myself it's like being locked out of my own house.

Because of the freedom and liberation, I have found in my continued practice of staying connected with my sexual experiences and my own sexuality, my wish for you is to be free in your sexuality so that you can access the magic and alchemy of sex. It is nothing to be afraid of. It is to be honored, loved, enjoyed, and revered.

Jeni Grace

Life Coach & Feminine Mentor
JLOZANOTELLI@GMAIL.COM

Returning to your Wild nature is not about negating, diminishing, or killing off the civilized parts of you that allow you to move and work within society. It is about allowing the wilder instincts, the untamed creative expression, and the natural intuition of your being to rise, guide, and direct your behavior and actions.

It takes courage to embrace the Wild feminine as your true home. It takes both grace and humility to love every part of yourself, not just the things that have been deemed culturally acceptable. When you are willing to honor your Wild nature, your feminine sexuality, your core sensual essence, and your true being by accepting and embracing every part of who you really are, you free the parts of yourself that bring about the greatest joy, pleasure, bliss, and unconditional love. What's more is, you free the woman next to you so she can do the same.

There is no single "right way" to be a woman. Your Wild femininity can take on many forms and none of them are wrong. Unless, of course, you are being inauthentic, in which case you have abandoned yourself and are no longer adding to the world the unique, artistic expression that it needed. *You* are the art the world needs to see, feel, and experience. Not a pretended, pruned, or programmed version of what would have otherwise been extraordinary.

Chiara's Story

CHIARA MECOZZI

Woman Be Wild, Featured Artist

Disentangling self-worth- one of the most important determinants of happiness, and priorities of life.

How can one be happy without self-love, the true unconditional love of oneself?

Well, you can't. Believe me, I tried.

Ever since I can remember, my priority was to make sure that everyone around me was happy. I worked so hard to always be a good daughter and for people to like me. The latin culture that I was brought up in tells women to serve that role from a young age. As I started cognitively understanding interactions and relationships with my family and peers, I internalized that as long they were happy, I was happy. I depended on their approval to make me feel like I was valued, worthy, accepted, and loved.

As my body started to develop throughout my teenage years, my self-esteem and self-worth got worse. Always caring too much about what others thought about me, I tried to look pretty, tried to follow trends, and tried to get attention. I compared myself to others and was constantly telling myself that I wasn't good enough, or smart enough, or skinny enough, or pretty enough, or had big enough breasts. Eventually I started living in constant anxiety, crumbling under the weight of my insecurities, and emotionally exhausted from caring so much about others' opinions.

Now that I think back on it, it baffles me how much power I gave them over my own happiness.

As a result, I ended up in very toxic relationships – relationships that were manipulating, abusive (both sexually and verbally), with narcissistic, unreliable, and unstable men.

In one such relationship, my partner coerced me into doing things I didn't feel comfortable doing, but because his opinion meant everything, I gave him all the power to decide if I was enough. When he wasn't happy with the weight I'd gained from grief after my brother's passing, he pushed me to go on a diet. He convinced me to take lewd photographs for him, and as uncomfortable as I was to go through with it, I did. I just shut my brain and did what he asked. The worst part of it was that he later used them to seduce other men online while he was impersonating me.

I spent a very long time and immeasurable energy allowing anything he wanted to happen, just to feel like I was worth something. And I convinced myself I wanted those things too – I was that scared of being rejected. Instead of feeling any sense of self-worth, I became more and more insecure and disconnected with myself, to the point that I didn't know who I was anymore, I was numb. I craved his attention. I craved anything that would make me feel loved, wanted, or worthy. The more he mistreated me, the more his opinion mattered.

I didn't know how to set boundaries or say no.

I didn't know how to walk away.

I found myself in states of debilitating depression, not knowing how to live.

I've had several relationships like that – some worse, some not that bad, but all in which I found myself putting my self-worth on others.

I eventually got married and although we loved each other so much, our relationship was very unstable. When we started dating, he was in a very insecure place, had just recently broken up, and I was coming out of a rollercoaster of a relationship. We were both young, and although it was very hard and destructive, we always figured out a way to stay together.

Throughout our relationship our dynamic consisted of him being very distracted by work, side businesses, and social life, and me trying to fit myself in there, figuring out my career, while also trying to be a good partner. I would do anything to be a part of his life, but I felt I was always fighting – fighting for his time, for security, and for stability. Yet the more I fought for these things, the more I spent my energy on everything he was doing, and the less on me.

I wasn't strong enough to just focus on what I needed and not care about what he was or wasn't doing. I think I knew deep down that focusing inward would help me, but I just couldn't do it. I wanted to, so much, but I was too weak. I tried so many times, and so many times I failed. I can't tell you how often I found myself crying in my closet with the lights out, not knowing how to get out of the dark hole I had fallen into.

I found myself living a very harmful, unpredictable, and unreliable life, with him prioritizing work and other relationships, and me waiting for him to give me the space in his life as his wife.

Again I found myself putting all my self-worth on someone else rather than myself. My goals, my ambitions, my happiness depended on making sure that I was fulfilling everything he needed.

I started getting very sick from the constant stress and anxiety I dealt with. I was fighting every day to be heard, to be understood, to be loved, by him and by me, and again I found myself in a place where the more I fought, the emptier

I felt. We failed to build the foundation we needed in order to face life together and to communicate our needs. So when it finally became unbearable for us both, we decided to separate.

At this point I found myself living alone in New York city in an apartment that I couldn't afford and without a stable job. My anxiety took its toll on my body, and I became very ill from all the stress. Some days I could hardly sit up from the pain in my neck and back.

I was at the lowest point in my life.

I was disconnected entirely from who I was, from my body, from my heart, and from my being. I found myself with two choices: fighting or giving up.

It is in this moment of desperation that I finally woke up and started climbing out of the abyss. I realized that everything I had been fighting for didn't matter anymore – all their opinions and their thoughts and all the weight I'd put on them, just left me. All the noise went away, I felt hope, I felt strength and I felt liberated. And it was then, finally, that I began to care about getting to know myself and fighting for who I really am.

This is when Brenda, my first autobiographical photograph was created.

This was the moment I found myself living and caring for nobody else but myself.

The woman in the photograph is a representation of me, in my most raw and vulnerable state, realizing that I no longer had to live for anyone else. I wasn't going to care what others thought about me, I was done. No one else mattered but me.

Ever since then, I haven't stopped creating. I dedicated almost two years to expressing myself about what I was going through with my photography. Since I was living in New York alone and figuring out how to survive, photography was my main medium and source of income. I couldn't find time for painting, and back then I didn't feel like I could've painted anyway, since I was still getting to know myself. I was still healing, learning, and unlearning.

My juxtaposed photographs became autobiographies of moments and emotions I was trying to understand and heal.

For example, Dominika, is my interpretation of the language between men and women. The men in my life have always loved cars, their power, their speed, and the identity behind owning them. Women have always been a shadow of that world.

That year, 2018, I created over 18 autobiographical pieces, but since I was still trying to figure out who I was, I found myself having a hard time using myself in the photographs. I used models from previous shoots, my sister, and people that I photographed, because using myself was just too hard. I was still so disconnected from my body, I didn't have the strength to really see myself.

Through journaling every morning, researching, reading countless books, watching videos, and listening to seminars by Brene Brown, Esther Perel, and Eckhart Tolle among others, I started noticing a shift in the way I was living.

I started approaching life differently, I slowly started trusting – trusting myself and trusting the universe.

I began creating very genuine connections with the most wonderful and supporting people. People who stood up for me, even against myself. What really amazed me is that most of them were women. Women who didn't know me, women who trusted me and stood by my side, helped me with my career, pushed my limits and always believed in me.

That's not to say every day was easy – I was still prone to intense bouts of lowness, anxiety, uncertainty, and pain. But trusting the universe has a way of giving you the things you need in life, and when you least expect them.

One day, I was coming home from Madrid to New York, and I had a layover in Lisbon. For the whole two hours I waited for that second flight home, I cried from anguish. Not only was I leaving my sister behind, but I was dealing with situations and conversations surrounding my separation and I was still feeling so much pain from it all. There was so much work I had yet to do to find peace within myself with everything that had happened.

As I was standing in the middle of the transit lounge, sad, lost, and alone, a lady came up to me to see if I was okay. I could barely stand up. In that moment, as I looked into her eyes, and saw my reflection in them, something inside of me just clicked.

I told her I was okay, and thanked her for asking me, and

I ran to the bathroom. I looked at myself in the mirror, and in that moment I told myself, "no more." No more crying. No more pain. No more desperation. So I washed my face, put makeup on, and as I walked back out into the world I promised to start a new life for myself.

As I got my bags and walked up to the gate to board my flight, I looked up and this guy was standing there, looking at me, with a big smile on his face. We only had five minutes to exchange pleasantries on the shuttle to the plane. He told me he lived in San Francisco, was a French teacher, and was a drummer, I told him I was from Argentina and lived in New York and was an artist. Then we exchanged contacts as we boarded, and that was it. In that moment I was so focused on me, I was so raw and vulnerable, that I didn't even have the head or heart space to understand what the universe was doing. I didn't think much of it and went on with my life.

Being in New York with this newfound sense of determination and boundaries I had set up for myself, I finally got to understand what peace, stability, self-love, and security feel like.

I felt free. I felt alive. I felt like I could breathe.

I felt so much strength within my body and heart, that with that feeling, the photograph, "The Only Way" was born. The first photograph that I exposed myself in. And I felt EMPOWERED.

I didn't care what anyone thought. What that photograph made me feel, no one else had ever made me feel, and I had created it. It came from within me.

I spent a year focusing on getting to know myself profoundly. Journaling became a daily habit and the most incredible way of understanding who I was. Through journaling I have been able to learn, clarity and heal many past traumas. Still to this day I journal every day and I'm still learning and healing.

I also learned to face my fears. Every time a challenge arose that made me feel uncomfortable, I would face it. It was the only way to become stronger.

During all this time, that guy from the plane and I messaged each other and got to know each other more and more. For me, it was still very hard to trust someone, or even to love again. But he was different, and so was I. We decided to start dating long distance – it was the only way I felt I could be with someone. I still needed more time for myself.

We dated for one year, a year during which I learned so much about myself by being alone, and also by being with someone who understood me, treated our relationship as his priority, and who made me feel safe. For the first time, I was able to feel what stability with another person meant: for once, our relationship was easy.

You know the phrase "Be with someone who makes you want to be a better person"? Well, I finally figured out what it meant.

If you're going to be with anyone at all it shouldn't just be with someone who constantly tells you that you are amazing as you are, or who wants you to be better or happy for yourself

– these things matter, of course, but it's much more than that.

Be with someone who doesn't bring chaos and uncertainty into your life.

Be with someone who helps you feel secure and stable in your relationship.

Be with someone who makes life easy, so that you can focus all your energy into being present and at peace, and into fulfilling your passion and your work.

That's the kind of partner who inspires you to wake up each day wanting to be better.

After that year and after getting to know each other and feeling so much love and certainty, we decided to move to Lisbon together. Living in Europe had been in my plans all my life, so I trusted my intuition and the opportunity that was put in front of me. I trusted myself and trusted the universe, and we moved in together.

I sold everything that I owned. I wanted to start a new life, disconnected from all the material things that I had once thought made me happy. I sold and donated dresses, purses, furniture, jewelry, clothes, and so many things I had accumulated from my past life. I got rid of everything. I felt liberated. The less I cared for material things, the more I could see and love myself.

Almost immediately after I moved to Lisbon, Covid and Lockdown happened. I kept journaling and through my writing, I decided to use the time in lockdown to learn more about myself, grow, forgive myself, and heal. The universe was giving the whole world a pause to reconnect with our inner being and love.

With everything I'd learned, being in lockdown at this stage of my life gave me the space to address long-cultivated issues with my own body. One day in particular, I got out of the shower and started spiraling down a particularly deep rabbit hole of self-hatred when I looked in the mirror. This couldn't go on, I told myself.

I decided to use my photography and painting to figure this out. I decided I was going to take photos of myself and paint myself to figure out how to love my body.

I set up the tripod and immediately started taking nude photographs of myself – it was probably one of the hardest things I'd ever done. The only other time I had done this wasn't with my own will. At first, I was very shy and discouraged and I felt pain, but I kept going. I wasn't going to stop. I was going to change the way that I thought about myself, by seeing myself. I was not my vagrant, hateful thoughts. I was done listening to that voice. I was going to love my body.

After going through the photographs, I set up a canvas on two chairs and started sketching my body onto the canvas.

It was so hard to complete the first painting of this series, I couldn't even include my head. Just my body. I used very washed-out colors, and was fighting myself throughout the whole process, but as I stepped back, my whole body started vibrating.

When I looked upon the painting, I felt so much strength. I felt liberated, and something else I had never felt before: I felt love for myself.

From that moment, I didn't stop painting. Every week I was creating a new oil painting. I decided to go even bolder. Make the colors and contrast darker, show my body in a more emboldened and empowered way. I felt a very genuine connection with myself and so much awareness in my body. I felt my whole-body vibrating. I cried, I laughed, I danced, I got turned on, I painted with my emotions, with my energy, with my sex, with my love, and with my light.

One of the most powerful artworks of this series is "Free, Together, We Bloom". During the process of painting this piece, I had never felt so connected with my inner self. I wasn't painting with my mind, my thoughts, or my program, I was painting with my energy, my presence, and my light. I was physically transmitting what my body felt in that moment, and it made sense. I felt I was communicating and vibrating with the paint, the figures in the canvas, and the colors. I have never felt so in tune with my inner Being.

The experience of that painting was so enlightening, I wanted to feel more of it, so I decided to go even bigger.

I was disentangling so many years of self-hate, self-sabotage, programmed behavior, and liberating myself from all of it.

And I keep doing it every day.

I'm still healing, I'm still learning, I'm still unlearning, and I'm still forgiving myself and others.

But what I do know now is that I am worthy.

I am PODEROSA.

PODEROSA

Chiara Mecozzi

Fine Artist & Photographer

@CHIARAMECOZZI

ART@CHIARAMECOZZI.COM

Acting as something other than who and what you are is suppression of self and soul. Suppression is the opposite of love. Suppression hides and defies. Love sees and frees. When you hide your true nature (thereby hiding yourself and your soul), you prevent true connection with everything and everyone. You become isolated, locked inside your hiding place, shriveling up, shutting down, and slowly, quietly, you die. Your body may continue to walk and talk, but inside, *you* are gone.

Christina's Story

Some of my earliest memories are filled with shame. I remember being taunted because of how flirtatious of a child I was, because of the clothing I wanted to wear, because I didn't look like other girls my age. I remember my body developed young and I felt immense shame for not looking like every other girl in my grade. In church, there would be days when my skirt was 'too short' and I'd be given clothing to wear underneath it or on the rare, humiliating occasion teachers would pull my skirt down or cover me with blankets. I remember feeling like I was too much, too big, too expressive, too emotional.

All of this got worse when I realized I was queer. I had spent my whole life believing that sex before marriage was a sin next to murder when you add the aspect of homosexuality the shame doubled. I spent a lot of time running. pretending. hiding.

Every day was a constant effort to make myself smaller. Less noticeable, while still craving to be seen. I felt like there was a war inside of me and I had nowhere to aim the fire but at myself. I developed an eating disorder and a self-harm habit. Death fascinated me and so did depression. Many summer nights of my childhood were spent laying in the driveway of my parent's house and wishing I was anyone else.

It definitely got worse before it got better. When I left home I went to a church school because I knew it would make my family happy. It made sense. It felt familiar and safe. I drove from San Diego up to a tiny town in Idaho where the sun almost never shines during the school year. I spiraled. Still in the closet, still dealing with untreated mental illness but this time I also had 16 credits to attend to and an endless stream of people who needed me just as much as I needed someone. I simultaneously had to be the mother to all of my friends who were equally as depressed and keep myself alive. During that time I drove three of my friends to the hospital after suicide attempts. My mental health was dismal and I was developing every bad coping mechanism I could find. I felt like I was a slave to my life and there were a few nights where I considered who would miss me if I was gone. I let people who had horrible intentions for me into my life because I didn't have the energy to tell them no. I was abused and I felt like I was outside of myself watching my body and my sexuality be stolen away from me. I crawled further and further into my shell until it felt like I wasn't even real anymore. My anxiety and depression had me in a haze that no one seemed to be able to pull me out of. More importantly, I couldn't help myself.

Two heartbreaking years later I left. I ran. this time, however, it was in a good direction. I got away from a church that told me I couldn't be who I am. I ran away from people who hurt me and abused me. I ran to the unknown and moved to somewhere completely new. I came out. My parents mourned me as part of their "eternal family". I got letters and emails and messages from what seemed like everyone I knew in the church telling me that I was a sinner. My brother told me he wished I had been "comfortable enough to stay in the closet". All of this hurt, but not nearly as much as the pain of being inauthentic. I wore short skirts, and then ditched dresses in general because I realized I have always hated them. I stopped doing what people wanted me to do and started doing what felt right. I dated women, I had amazing sex, I dyed my hair pink, and then black, and then pink again. I started ending relationships with people who didn't want what was best for me. I focused on my art and my photography and I eventually manifested a full-time business for myself doing what makes me happy to be alive. I started going to therapy and doing yoga. I stopped all of my bad coping mechanisms and replaced them with as much love as I could possibly give myself. I had so many years to make up for.

I found my tribe but more importantly, I found myself. I had been there all along.

I am a strong and beautiful queer woman who spends her days making people feel beautiful. If someone had told me as I was laying on my parent's driveway with tear-stained cheeks, that I would be this happy one day, I wouldn't have believed them. There is still the darkness but it doesn't own me. Every time I tap into my power it fades more and more.

Every time I listen to my body and feed it the food it needs, it fades. Every time I listen to my intuition and only spend time with those who deserve it, it fades. I'm learning it's all about listening. Not distracting, not numbing, listening. I am freer now than I have ever been. Every day I shed more and more of the rules that I have placed on myself. I let myself play like the kid I never got to be. I let myself blossom into the woman that has been waiting for me this whole time.

My religion is empathy and love. I use the pain I've been through to make people feel less alone. I use it to make art and as a reminder to always stand up for myself. My past is something I shed more and more every day. It doesn't own me. I am free.

Christina Mellor

Freelance Photographer

@CHRISTINASCAPTURES

WWW.CHRISTINASCAPTURES.COM

"Nature does not ask permission. Blossom and birth whenever you feel like it."

— Clarissa Pinkola Estés

I want to remind you that no matter how deadened you may feel, you are divine. You are here to express that divinity in human form. To embody your divinity, you must be willing to embrace your humanity. You must embrace **what it means for you** to be a woman. Your divine spirit wants to be expressed physically. It is why you are here. You are here to give life to your divine being as a human, and specifically, as a woman. Above all else, you came to physically embody the Wild Woman (Goddess) within. You are not here to be tamed, controlled, or defined by others, you are here to be your own unique expression of Her.

So many people are trying to define who women should and shouldn't be, creating conflicting poles of unnecessary tension that falsely define and label what a "real woman" is and is not. On one side, some still cling to the repressive patriarchal tradition that a woman should only be a stay-at-home mom, to cook, clean, and take care of children with no role outside the home, not part of the workforce, and in many ways, subservient to men. On the other side, there are those who want to overthrow the "rule of men" replacing the patriarchy with a matriarchy. These radical feminists, as they compete with men, create the opposite imbalance as they abandon one their true femininity in favor of masculinity.

We see these as competing opposites when really, they are two extremes of the same spectrum. While these two extremes tend to garner all the attention and would like us to think they are the only choices, the vast majority of women fall somewhere in the countless variations between. Often we are shamed by other women to take a certain position or definition, but why must we tell each other how we should express our femininity? This is as absurd as saying we should all be roses and there is no room for daisies.

A wild and natural state of being is not totally chaotic, though it does include chaos. It is also not a total state of order, although it does include order. Your natural wild state is a state of balance; balanced being, balanced feeling, and balanced expression. The Wild is limitless because it includes everything; light, dark, young, old, pleasure, pain, joy, grief, order, chaos, peace, turmoil, creation, and destruction. You are a limitless being because you too are made to have, feel, be, and express all of these things.

The only way we can truly return to our natural untamed state is to accept and embrace every aspect of ourselves and each other. What we cannot accept in ourselves, we project onto others. What we cannot embrace in ourselves, we fear in others. This throws us out of balance and keeps us spinning in judgements of right versus wrong, good versus bad, better versus worse. When we learn to love, accept and balance these energies within ourselves, we heal and balance the world. What profound power we have on this earth plane when we choose to embody the wholeness of Love by allowing space for all to be.

How freeing it is when we stop trying to define femininity and feminine power as one extreme or the other. Women are many things, feminine energy shows up in many ways, and they are all beautiful. You decide what feminine is in your own expression. Instead of defining what a woman is, perhaps we should *undefine* what a woman is. Defining something traps and limits it. If there is one thing certain about the nature of true feminine power, it is that it is completely undefinable, unlimited, free, and Wild.

Love yourself as you are. Whatever form femininity takes in your authentic expression, is perfect. It is unique and because of that, it is needed. Your unique and individual feminine expression is a crucial part of what allows feminine nature and power to remain unlimited and undefinable. The moment you try to be what others say you should be, you become less than your true self, a limited, stunted, and crippled parody defined by someone else's terms. By removing all externally imposed definitions, you become truly feminine; undefined, unbridled, and unlimited. You become Wild.

This is your nature. Some see it as chaos, I see it as freedom.

PAINTING 24

SEX AND SEXUALITY

"If we are really going to be sexually liberated, we need to make room for a range of options as wide as the variety of human desire. We need to allow ourselves the freedom to figure out what we internally want from sex instead of mimicking whatever popular culture holds up to us as sexy. That would be liberation."

—Ariel Levy

Cultural opinions about feminine sexuality range from accusing women of being prudish and mean for withholding sex, to being scheming and manipulative for using their sexuality to seduce and gain power. These skewed and extreme perspectives steer us away from seeing the reality that women, even more than men, have a natural and innate desire to express and enjoy their sexuality.

A double standard of sexual morality exists condemning sexual activity for women while condoning it for men. We have made women objects of sexual desire but then expect them to be chaste and pure. While men are taught to embrace their sexuality, even flaunt it, women are taught to hide and deny their sexual nature. One of the most shameful insults to a man is the accusation that he is not getting enough sex. For a woman, it is that she is sexually too loose or too easy. For a man, having sex with a lot of women is encouraged, admired, congratulated, and even celebrated, "what a stud!" For a woman, it is shamed, "what a slut!"

Is this really the culture we want? Is it really the story we want to tell?

To address this glaring inconsistency, some elements of society simply condemn and shame sexuality altogether as sinful or evil. These puritanical crusaders would deprive or severely limit both men and women of their natural capacity to enjoy sexual pleasure, by diminishing our ability to appreciate and embrace the natural beauty in our human sexuality, thus, keeping us from living the life we truly desire.

Many people are trapped in this suppressive conditioning without realizing it because it is so normalized in our culture. But normal doesn't mean good, or even healthy. We can simply accept the 5,000 years of patriarchy and the cultural conditioning we were born into, or we can choose to take responsibility for our part in accepting and perpetuating these repressive and crippling beliefs and values. We can own up to the fact that our internal thoughts and beliefs do in fact create our external experience, and that if we continue to carry these repressive patterns within ourselves, we will never be free. Not only that, but we will perpetuate the damage and keep future generations locked inside the same prison.

If you have a culture that convinces women that they are less interested in sex than men, when in fact the opposite is more often true, you set women up to feel deviant for having sexual feelings and desires. Shame storms in, leading to denial and suppression, and a host of psychological issues ensue. It is insanity to continue down this road. It is time we turn around.

Much of our sexual shame develops because of what we have learned to believe about our bodies. Supporting only one shape, one size, one color, one form is to ignore and discount the beauty of nature. In the same way that there cannot be one kind of flower, one kind of tree, one kind of canyon, lake, ocean, insect, beast, or bird- there cannot and will never be one kind of woman. We must reject any idea that tells us otherwise. Do not cheat yourself of the strength and confidence that comes with being unique and different.

Emphasis on the hope or wish for a different size, shape, color, or form, puts your sexuality and thereby your soul, to sleep. Instead, turn your attention to your feminine nature, creativity, and expression. No matter how the female body appears or manifests, it is the vehicle for embodying divine feminine energy, creating and giving life, and expressing fierce love and passion.

Our culture values the body for its beauty and traps the idea of beauty into one form. If we believe that our bodies must look a certain way in order for them to be deemed beautiful or desirable, we spend most of our lives wishing we were someone else. Notice what a severe disconnection this would cause a woman to have from her own body, her individual sexuality, and her feminine power. The Wild values the body for its ability to feel and frees it to exist in all forms. We must stop asking ourselves, "does it fit?" and instead ask, "does it feel?" Your body is not separate from you and your experience. Rather, it is what allows for all of your experience while on Earth. It is what carries your soul through this life and acts as a teacher, mentor, guide, and friend. Your body is not "supposed to be" anything but exactly what it is. The real work is not to change it, but to feel it in every capacity which can only be done through love, acceptance, and presence.

There is no right or better size, shape, color, or physical expression. I am not here to say that your physical health and performance is not important. It is, but not in the ways we are taught it is. The shape of our bodies is a by-product of the way we move and eat, not the reason we should be moving or eating a certain way. The reason we need to pay attention to what we eat and how we move is that it opens and expands our body's capacity to feel. Moving our bodies and feeding them naturally, increases our ability to connect with our body and all its senses. What a waste it is to wonder or worry if our bodies are thin enough, tall enough, small enough, curved enough, or good enough. The real questions are, does it feel pleasure and joy? Is it connected to the heart and soul? Does it move, dance, laugh, and play? And do I allow for all of these things to flow through me? Nothing else matters. Take your body back.

Like our female bodies and our feminine nature, our

sexuality cannot be confined to a single rigid form, but instead, depends on your individual, authentic expression to deepen and thrive. Your sexuality is your life-force. All of life finds expression purely and effortlessly within sexual experience. We can be more alive, more awake and more aware while expressing our sexuality than anything else in life.

Sex and each individual's unique sexuality is a microcosm of life's experiences. Our sexual experiences contain all the aspects of life that we struggle with, yearn for, strive to understand, desire to make peace with, and are learning to accept. If we are conscious and aware during our sexual experiences, we will find all of life's treasures and challenges mirrored back to us.

When I was 20-years-old, I got married. Culturally, this was very normal. Where I grew up, it was celebrated and to some degree expected for girls to marry early. The first time I had sex was on my wedding night. My sexual education mostly included directions like, "don't have sex until you're married" and, "giving sex to your husband when he wants it makes you a good wife." Looking back, I cringe a little. At the time, however, though it made me feel uncomfortable, I didn't know any different. Even then, I felt something was missing. My sexual experience in that marriage wasn't negative, but it wasn't positive. It lacked luster and emotional connection. What I know now, is that I was experiencing my relationship with myself through my relationship with sex. I was completely disconnected from my feminine roots and because of that, I was disconnected from my body, my desires, and my partner. I see now how this disconnection did not begin and end in the bedroom. Being disconnected from my sexuality meant I was disconnected from my entire life. The most devastating part of this was that I had no idea. It is not something we are taught to be aware of.

What followed was a marriage that dwindled, and ultimately ended with my then-husband seeking both emotional and sexual connection elsewhere. Afterward, I took time to heal and to redefine myself and what I wanted in life. As I started to date again, I had to completely strip myself of every belief and idea that had been instilled (programmed) by my parents, teachers, peers, and religion surrounding sex. I knew that I wanted a different experience with sex and that in order to have it, my feelings and beliefs about sex had to change too. I had to redefine my relationship with sex. What was right, wrong, good, bad, better, or worse? Was it really wrong to have sex outside of marriage? Was it wrong to have multiple partners? Was it actually better with men, or would sex with a woman be equally fulfilling? I decided to put my faith in my own feelings and experiences instead of blindly following the direction of someone else. I began to trust my own inner authority. This set me free of all expectations. It put me back in charge of my own body, my own mind, and my own outcome.

I was shocked when sex with a man I hardly knew felt more emotionally connected than it ever had in my previous serious relationship. What was different? The only thing I could come up with was me. *I* was different. I had to understand more about what was going on in both my internal world and my external experience. That moment set me on a path to discover something I innately knew was missing from both my sexual and overall experience: self-connection and self-realization.

Without fully understanding what compelled me to move down this path, I continued. I became intensely curious about my sexuality and sensual expression. I was fascinated by how it seemed to awaken something in me that had been put to sleep. Something I needed. Something I loved. Something that made me, *me*. I know now that it was my soul calling me back to the Wild. For five years my entire experience seemed to revolve around sex, sexuality, sensuality, my body, my femininity, and intimate connections of all kinds. Sex became my teacher. It was the most beautiful, exciting, painful, powerful, frustrating, inspiring, and expansive experience of my life.

My 20's were full of sexual experimentation and liberation. It was a quest for freedom. At the time, I thought I was just "having fun." What I know now is that there was a lot more at play. My body became my personal guide and tool as I pushed my own boundaries and confronted every piece of sexual shame I had acquired from my upbringing. I dressed in whatever made me feel beautiful, I had sex with other women, had sex with multiple partners, with people I'd never known, with people I'd known for a long time, and with myself.

For a time, each of these sexual encounters brought up deeply buried fear and shame of what it meant to be "good", what it meant to be "happy", and what it meant to be a woman. Sex stripped me bare in soul as often as it did in body and quickly became my greatest teacher and most honest ally. It taught me how to speak up for myself, how to communicate my needs and desires, how to sink back into my own body, how to let myself feel good, how to let myself be seen, and how to give from my heart. It taught me how to confront my own shadow, how to peel back layers of fear that were never mine, and how to see other people in a real, raw, and compassionate way.

It didn't take long for me to learn to choose partners based on the energy they carried and whether or not they shared a mutual desire for sincere connection. It was amazing how my experience changed as I chose my partners based on what I felt in my body rather than what I saw with my eyes. It taught me how to trust and use my intuition and more subtle senses rather than relying solely on what was logical or visible.

Sex, our most Wild, natural urge and desire, was the gateway to my sensual awakening. It was how I reconnected and reclaimed my wild feminine nature. It was the key to unlocking my personal freedom. The only thing that made this possible was my present participation with what was going on in my internal world. I asked a lot of questions, I read new books, and I sat still and quiet for long periods of time using my own experience as a standard of truth, which allowed me to eradicate the stories I had been told by parents, teachers, coaches, television, and magazines growing up.

The more I tore away the layers of conditioning surrounding my sensual and sexual expression, the more I was able to surrender to my own joy and pleasure by following the path back to my individual truth. My creativity heightened, my relationships were more authentic and fulfilling, and I began to live in bliss because I had freed myself from fears and limitations set by others.

Your pain is the gateway to your joy. Joy is created when we consciously and energetically transmute our most difficult experiences into our greatest points of power. The pain of repressed feminine sexuality and sensuality was my gateway back into the Wild. There are countless gateways and none are more powerful than the other. What gives a gateway its power, is when you choose it as your personal teacher and guide. When you commit to walking through its fire, you earn the life you are meant to live.

Ivy's Story

I'm Ivy Wolfe. And my story starts in a closet.

At age 13, I was taken out of public school, everything I owned sorted and most of it taken from me. I was put in a closet for 3 years. The reason? Sexual Shame. My mother, bless her wounded heart, was filled with fear, and her first born began developing sexually, the wild child I was, now moved into a wild WOMAN. Developing, sexual, wild. So in the closet I went. I found an immovable power in that closet, an untakeable thing. I astral projected, I had sex with ghosts. My safety was our property; I was initiated by my only friends, the trees, the wind, the grass, the dirt, the creatures of the earth. I explored my body, my mind, my heart, the sky. I climbed trees and collected leaves in my hair. And eventually, one day, I was let out of the closet. Rooted into the immoveable wildness of one's untameable soul. I was finally free.

I left home.

The reason I was put in a closet, was for the breathtaking sensual photos I had posted on the internet.

So I sought to reclaim this experience, my body, my sex, my sensuality.

I sought out modeling, and eventually, I sought to take my clothes off again.

Trembling, one sunny day in Portland on a nude beach, I asked the photographer if he'd mind taking photos of me with my clothes off.

In his safety, I flew. My clothes dropped to the ground, and so did all my shame.

I looked around, I looked down at my naked body, and all the naked bodies around me. I wept. I leapt for joy. I scratched my legs as I climbed trees and posed fully nude in the place that held me through those years. Nature. Momma. I howled at the moon as I frolicked naked all day until it dipped under the ocean for the night.

I reclaimed myself that day.

I was a shy girl, I wouldn't dance or sing in front of

people, I was anxious, nervous, and deeply lacking confidence.

I quit my job. I started stripping. I faced the shame that brought my mom to put me in that closet, with an open, hurting, human, courageous heart. I faced the shame that had dulled me, silenced me, scared me into submission.

I dealt with family abandoning me, and I continued to reach for those voices of encouragement, of shamelessness, of wholeness embodied.

I became an award winning, magazine cover gracing PORNSTAR.

To me, it was the biggest way i could communicate to myself, to everyone else, just how fucking FREE we actually were.

I found a place where my sex was worshipped, instead of shoving it into a closet.

I broke down many times. Not everyone approved. I fell to the floor of my entire self many times, and broke into a million shattered rejected pieces.

And again and again I have picked myself up, pulled back all fragments and lovingly glued it back together with the blood of my moon and the juice of my pleasure.

I ventured deeper into sex work, innately discovering it was about so much more then sex. I was a safe place for the wild, for the real, for the raw, for the human, for others to come out. That was why I was there. That was why I was hired. To hold the space for acceptance of the wild, what wild really means. What's Wild is what's naturally occurring in that moment, unwithheld. As all of life exists in this way, the wild is simply life in its rawest form. And it is our natural state of being.

I provide this space. I give this permission slip. I wave this flag.

So if you ask what led me back to my true center, what got me here, and what I'd say to other women in closets of their own.

Every time you hear your wild whispering in your ears, listen deeper. Follow it until you question your sanity. Until you are laughing in the ultimately chaotic colors of life unfiltered, unwithheld, and WILD. Everytime you see yourself go to hold back, push in. Everytime you go to silence yourself, scream. Everytime you go to cover yourself, yank it all off. Everytime they tell you that you can't, every judgement they throw at you, hear it as a cry for help. Love yourself so deeply, so unwavering, that you allow yourself to wander into the deepest depths of wildness of your own roaming, moaning, glowing soul. Be a lighthouse for others drowning in their own self judgement. Find the immoveable peace and satisfaction of following your own compass, and throw out the one they gave you.

If something scares you, do it.

Just do it.

Stop thinking. That's how they trap you, you are wild, you are Woman. Leave the logic for the masculine.

It's really that simple.

Do it Woman.
Do it.

Ivy Wolfe

Musician, Artist
@OFFICIALIVYWOLFE

What my feminine awakening and sexual liberation have shown me, is that sex and each individual's unique sexuality is a microcosm of our life's experiences. Our sensual and sexual experiences, no matter how small, shed light on the aspects of life we struggle with, yearn for, and strive to understand. Sexuality teaches us about our desire for belonging, our need to be loved, to be seen, to be heard, and our level of willingness to show and experience vulnerability, courage, excitement, pleasure, pain, acceptance, unpredictability, fear, uncertainty, loss, comfort, and joy.

There is a richness, fullness, and wholeness to life that we reclaim when we remove the ideas and limitations of others and replace them with personal truth found in honest, present experience. I am grateful for my upbringing, but I had to be willing to question it. I had to be willing to push religious boundaries and abandon cultural limits. Just like sex, the experience was a beautiful, magical mess.

Now, I get to spend my life helping women dis-member old, shameful ideas of what it means to be a sexually, sensually empowered woman, so that they can remember that it is, in fact, their birthright and their greatest gift.

By exploring your sexuality and fully embracing your unique sensual expression you catalyze a paradigm shift in every other area of your life.

+ Your willingness to fully express yourself between the sheets will manifest as a willingness to be who you really are out in the open.

+ Speaking up when something hurts during sex, will save you from being silent when you feel hurt in your life.

+ If you are willing and unafraid to tell your partner how to fulfill your sexual needs, you will be willing and unafraid to do what is necessary to fulfill your desires in your life.

+ If you say, "yes" but mean "no" in bed, you will do the same in the outside world and always feel that people take advantage of you, when it is you who has not made it clear what you will and will not take on.

Your sex life is a mirror of your daily life. It will give you the most intimate, and often the most uncomfortable window into what is really going on inside of you. The way you communicate, behave, express, think, and react during sex is a clear indication of how you will speak, act, move, believe, and respond in day-to-day activities. When we are disconnected sexually, we are disconnected totally.

"The behavior of a human being in sexual matters is often a prototype for the whole of his other modes of reaction in life."

– Sigmund Freud

The more you are disconnected from yourself as a sexual, sensual being, the more trapped you become in limitations that are suppressing and crippling to your true Wild self. Healing and transformation happens when we reject those limitations and reconnect to our natural, Wild state of being. Deep, meaningful, and attentive connection with your feminine sexuality is your path to freedom and empowerment in this world.

When Wild, erotic energy is harnessed, and when we are expressing our deepest sexual needs and desires, we experience an outpouring of life-force and power. We become vessels for our unique divine purpose and can use this creative energy to develop our communication skills, intuition, personal willpower, and emotional maturity, all of which are necessary to be in flow with the best this life has to offer.

We can be more alive, more awake, and more aware during sex than nearly anywhere else in life. We have all experienced deep joy in connection during sex, as well as deep pain from disconnection during sex. It is a beautiful, simple representation of the joy and pain available in every area of our lives, dependent on our ability and willingness to cultivate true and deep connection. Though mostly associated with sexual desire, sexual energy is creative energy and with it comes the deep longing for true connection, unity, and balance. Expressed sexuality is an intimate sharing of one's self in body, mind, and spirit. This, of course, is not confined to expression during sex. Your sexuality can and should be expressed in many areas of your life. Especially in your creative endeavors and expression.

Imagine the difference you would feel if sex was no longer used to mask emotions or abused to suppress your feminine sensuality, and instead was given its rightful place in our lives as an avenue for healing, growth, freedom, and awakening. This is not just about sex itself. You are not "sex-crazed" for giving this topic the time, attention, and energy it deserves. This is about reclaiming your life, your body, and your power. It is about owning who you are and what you can become, and learning to express your truth by connecting with your Wild nature. Ultimately, it is about you setting yourself free because no one else can do that for you.

When you repress your sexuality, your needs, desires, and the wildness inside you, you simultaneously dim and dull your creativity. You shut off the flow of creative life-force you were born to mold and shape. I am not suggesting that the solution is to overindulge and act out sexually with complete abandon. Overindulgence and carelessness with sexual energy and your natural sexuality can and will lead to destructive patterns such as unconsciously seeking outside attention to validate your self-worth. This will damage your own creative process as you leak and waste your creative life-force energy (feminine energy). Once you begin treating sex as an empowering personal practice that deserves your attention, honor, respect, and open, authentic enjoyment, you are automatically led back to your most Wild natural state.

Sexual freedom and empowerment does not mean having sex with anyone and everyone. In fact, it has far less to do with your partners and far more to do with your relationship with, understanding of, and love for your own sexuality, body, and being. It is about making the shift from external validation to internal fulfillment. Your body deserves your highest respect. When you respect your body, others will respect your body. Your body is intuitive and wise, and it will be your guide if you let it. You give your body its power back by trusting in its knowing. This is where all sexual healing begins; healing from the crippling psychological fear, shame, guilt, and pain caused by a lifetime of cultural suppression and condemnation. Your body can help you release all of that accumulated negative energy and let it go forever.

Diving deep into your sexuality is the fastest way to reclaim feminine freedom. As I said, this is not just about sex, though it certainly includes it (a lot of it). Sexuality is not even about seduction. It is about being in your own creative power, which is the most seductive thing you can witness in another person. Your sexuality is less about your behavior and more about your state of being. It is a primary component of who you are in alignment with your true nature.

"Sexuality is not a leisure or part-time activity.
It is a way of being."

— Alexander Lowe

In expressing your sexuality, how would you speak if there was no judgment? How would you dress if there were no social taboos? How would you move and act if there were no critics to shame you? What would you embody if you could be whatever you truly wanted? How would your Wild nature and sensual desires become a natural, exciting, and fulfilling part of your daily life?

As a woman, regardless of sexual preference, when you are cut off from your sexuality you are cut off from your power, your spirit, your art, your desire, and your joy as a muse for this world. Some forms of feminism insist that we take back power, but a masculine form of power, causing us to lose our wild feminine life-force. When we separate from this feminine power, we detach ourselves from our nature. Without this connection, we are less able to inspire and move the world.

"The woman's mission is not to enhance the masculine spirit, but to express the feminine; hers is not to preserve a man-made world, but to create a human world by the infusion of the feminine element into all of its activities."

– Margaret Thatcher

If you truly want freedom, you must release your fears surrounding your feminine sexuality and surrender to your Wild nature. By nature, you are free but were born into a world where you have been tamed and taught to suppress your innate power and presence.

Sex can be a powerful evolutionary tool because it shows us where we are on the path to self- realization; the fulfillment of our potential. It can help us overcome fear and limiting conditioning as we allow ourselves to experience and surrender to true physical and emotional joy. If you are experiencing any sort of fear, shame, guilt, lack of expression, a stifled voice, tension in the body, or overall denial of yourself and soul in the bedroom- you are without a doubt, experiencing the same things in your everyday life. When you allow yourself to experience full openness, freedom of expression, fearless desire, uninhibited pleasure and play, and devotion to your own needs and your partner's, you will begin to harness sexual energy, mindful presence, and flow in the bedroom that will spill into every other available life experience.

"Sexuality is one of the ways that we become enlightened, actually, because it leads us to self-knowledge."

— Alice Walker

Owning and exploring your sexuality is really about personal evolution; an awakening and embracing of your own Wild power. For years, I "performed" in the bedroom. Sex was not only a way of seeking validation from men, but was also a place I felt I had to look, sound, and behave a certain way to be considered "desirable" or "sexy". This had far less to do with the men I was with and far more to do with what my culture had taught me about my role in sex and romantic connection as a woman.

Fortunately, I eventually found myself with a partner who was present, sensitive, and aware enough to say, "Relax. You don't need to suck your stomach in." At that moment, I felt more seen and held than I ever had in my life. What they were really saying was, "Breathe. You're safe with me." It was such a simple moment, yet so powerful and profound. Its power came from my partner's willingness to speak and my willingness to respond authentically. From that point on I chose my sexual partners differently. I asked, "do I trust this person?" instead of, "does this person turn me on?" I learned that as women, we do not need to be "turned on" to have good sex. We need to be opened. It is still possible to have bad sex with a partner who "turns us on." But a partner who helps us feel safe, relaxed, and open... only good can come from that. This opening happens when our partner is gentle, patient, and worthy of our trust. We are opened by people who can hold us authentically in these intimate and vulnerable experiences. We open when we are seen and accepted. We open when we feel safe to love ourselves exactly as we are.

Since that day, I dropped the act in the bedroom and began to attract a different kind of partner into my life, a partner who was looking for a more meaningful, connected experience and who truly wanted what I brought to the experience, not what I had seen someone else bring to the bedroom on T.V. or in a porno. When I was having mediocre sex, it was never because the person I was with lacked anything. It was because I had a mediocre connection to my own sexuality. I lacked personal depth and intimacy. You can only connect, feel, experience, surrender to, and meet another person as deeply as you have connected with, felt, experienced, surrendered to, and met yourself.

Want to have better sex? Dive deeper. Cultivate personal trust and intimacy.

"Sexuality is not a thing, an act, or a behavior, but rather a state of being who you are, what your nature is."

— Julie McIntyre

How willing are we to express ourselves and our true desires? How willing are we to let go of fears and expectations so we can move past insecurity and into joy? Can we trust ourselves and our partner? Can we surrender to our Wild physical and emotional longing for connection so we can meet in the ultimate presence of love?

I have learned that in order for this to happen, we must eradicate our sexual shame and reclaim sexual freedom. There seems to be a misconception that our culture must change first before we can begin to live more freely in our sexuality. This is absolutely untrue. The only way a culture changes, is when individuals remember that the power to change lies always and only within them. Ask yourself, "Am I having the connected experiences and sexual fulfillment I want to have?" If the answer is no, only you have the power to change that. The same applies when you ask, "Am I living the life I want to live?"

Our culture has used morality to suppress our sexuality, but our sexuality is what makes life worth living. In fact, it is life itself. Returning to our Wild nature and embracing our feminine sexuality means that we must do more than agree that this is true. We must live as though we know it.

CULTURAL
CONDITIONING

Many women are trapped in lives that bear no resemblance to their true desires. I believe this is because there is a gap between who they have been told to be, and who they really are. This gap is in large part due to generations of social, political, and religious conditioning. Some of it intentional, some of it habitual. Be the woman who says, "this ends with me." It ends with your decision to direct your own life.

It is easy to think that your values, beliefs, hopes, and fears are uniquely your own. The reality is, the makeup of your mind has largely been shaped and molded by the social conditioning of your environment. It shapes your self-concept. It shapes your hopes and dreams, your fears and frustrations. It shapes how you feel about your past, and how you think about your future. How you think, feel and act is determined by the social/cultural conditioning your mind has undergone throughout your life. The majority of the pain in our lives stems from our passive willingness to believe and adopt this conditioning as truth.

"One believes things because one has been conditioned to believe them."

Aldous Huxley,
BRAVE NEW WORLD

From birth, we are indoctrinated into a model of femininity that reflects several millennia of patriarchal suppression and control. It is so entrenched, most of us don't even recognize it, let alone realize we have a choice to make.

Our souls cannot be led or fed by an unconscious culture. We cannot continue to move through life without questioning what we were programmed to believe as children. The same way foods have been modified by a genetic mutation to not express certain aspects of their natural state (i.e. original size, color, taste, etc), we are being modified through social and cultural conditioning that is being passed as "normal". We must remember that whether it be a human or a fruit, what in today's world is considered "normal" is not natural, and has dire consequences. Transcending cultural conditioning is not against your nature, it is against your training.

I first became aware of my own conditioned living and choices when I noticed that the lifestyle the Christian religion I, my family, and everyone who I knew was a part of, did not bring me the peace, comfort, or happiness that was promised or that I expected. These expectations were formed because of my belief in the stories, promises, and experiences of others who were sure that this particular religion was the only way to achieve full joy in this life. It is not wrong to rely on the stories and experiences of others, they can be helpful and inspiring, but they will only carry you forward for a time. Your Wild self will always push you to experience life in a unique and authentic way. To live a life of freedom, you are required to pave your own path.

In 2012, I remember looking around the room during a church meeting and asking myself, "Are these the people I want to model my life after? Does what I participate in and learn here make me happy?" "Do I feel inspired, passionate, and creative?" I immediately felt my answer was "no," so I stood up and left. It was the last church meeting I attended as an affiliated member of a religious organization. Afterwards, I remember writing down everything that made me feel uneasy about what I had been taught my whole life. Things like;

✦ We should feel shame when we make mistakes and be fearful of God's judgment unless we are perfectly obedient to a set of rules and regulations that someone has set down as His commandments.

✦ God is a "He" and somehow the greatest power in the universe does not require a "She".

✦ Only men are qualified to make decisions regarding spiritual worthiness and administer ordinances.

✦ There is only one path that leads to salvation and that all other paths lead to damnation.

✦ There are those who are "elect" before they are even born to become God's chosen people.

✦ Interracial relationships are somehow "lesser-than" and some races are superior to others.

✦ God punishes some of his children for eternity based on whether or not they keep his commandments in this brief lifetime.

✦ We must suppress sexual desire and only express it within very limited bounds (especially for women).

I brought the full list to my dad fully expecting him to explain away my questions. Instead, he calmly went over the list of grievances with me, shrugged, and agreed, "You're right. If you really feel this way, and you are unhappy, you are right to leave it all behind." As it turned out, he had been having similar thoughts and feelings. I immediately broke down into tears of shock and relief. Everything I had been taught to believe, everything I had considered as truth, was wiped away. It was now entirely up to me to feel and determine the best way to live my life.

It was lonely for a while. My entire network and community of friends, family, teachers, coaches, co-workers, and acquaintances belonged to and abided by this particular religion and its way of life. In the beginning, I felt awkward and uncomfortable as I started making different choices and shifting my beliefs and perception of what was right, wrong, good, bad, better, or worse. I had to redefine my entire reality. It was one of the most powerful things I have ever done.

"Happy people know that all the imperfections of the world are due to the conditioning of our minds which seeks perfection in the world according to the moral and statutory laws. Unless you free yourself from the binding of these rules and laws, there will hardly be any place for happiness in your life."

– Awdhesh Singh

As I paved my own path, I began to understand that there was no single "right" way of doing things. What was spiritually true for me looked different than what was true for some of my friends and family members, and that was okay! I learned to honor people's differences and to celebrate other ways of living. I learned to respect others' choices, and more importantly, I learned to respect my own choices no matter how they differ from those I love.

Redefining my path based purely on my own thoughts and feelings allowed me to establish a more sacred and meaningful connection with myself and with my higher power than I ever would have had, had I continued to sit in church meetings led by others. It took ripping myself out of the only environment

I had ever known to see and feel things clearly for myself. I lost friends, was criticized by people I looked up to, and felt less welcome in certain social circles. However, it was from this place that I was able to begin living in a full, connected, and authentic way. I also quickly met people who shared the same desire for authentic living. We were able to celebrate each other's unique paths and show each other real love and support.

Had I stayed and passively followed everything I was being taught instead of actively feeling and deciding what was right for me, I would have severely limited my capacity for growth and transformation. Choosing to deviate from what my cultural environment considered normal and right, is what allowed me to take my power back and become my own source of joy, love, peace, and freedom.

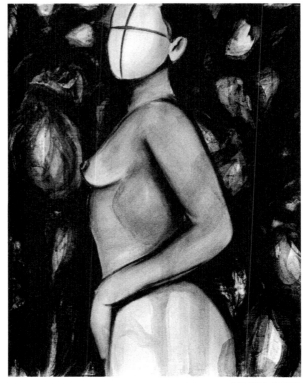

BY MY SIDE

Forget "bloom where you are planted". Plant yourself.
Rip yourself out of that root-bound pot and return to your Wild.
Stop waiting for the rain and go to the rain. Stop waiting for fertile
soil and move to fertile soil. Stop waiting for the sun to come out
and shine your own Light.
Then sink. Sink your wild roots back into
the depths of your own being.
Plant yourself into places, people, and feelings that allow your
roots to grow into the center of your heart and soul.

—Indigo

We seem to succumb to the pressure of the norm out of our desire to be accepted. Why do we allow ourselves to remain trapped in the harsh and limited reality that conditioning creates? Is it something we would naturally choose or is it because our culture, family, religion, community, government, etc. will not accept us if we do not abide by their "rules"? The latter feels more true to me. However, there comes a time where we must recognize that if we do not deviate from the norm, we can never progress or become totally ourselves or feel fully alive.

It is our personal change done on an internal level that will ultimately revolutionize the world we live in. Personal change precedes social change. They are inextricably linked. Imagine if there was personal, internal transformation happening to women around the world on a mass scale. Social and cultural change would be inevitable, and completely unstoppable. If enough of us return to our wild roots, reconnect with our hearts, and boldly step into the fullest expression of our souls, we will drive our world to it's edge, and quickly reach a tipping point that will change the trajectory of humanity forever.

What in your life has been predetermined, forced, or presented as "the only right way"? This is your chance to look at these things with a new understanding that you have a choice to make. You get to decide here and now whether or not to accept those things. As you clear out the ideas, beliefs, and behaviors that no longer serve you, you begin to forge your own path, pave your own way, and open infinite possibilities for yourself and future generations of women.

To help you get started, I will touch on how religious teachings, family traditions, political influence, the media, racial and national customs, and peer beliefs and values condition and limit us in ways we may not even be aware of. It is important to analyze each of these areas in your own life to see how they may be affecting you in ways you may not have previously considered.

Religious teachings

I have no interest in or reason to attack the idea of belonging to a religious organization or practicing and abiding by religious principles. I would, however, like to point out that many of us haphazardly follow and believe most, if not all of what we are taught in churches growing up because, well, it's the church! It must be true! We must also address the issue of religious organizations encouraging their members to follow with blind belief, "don't ask too many questions! Show some faith!" We gain the impression that to question the church is to question God. We are programmed with the belief that it is best to put all your faith in what religious teachers and organizations say, otherwise, God may punish you because you "knew better." But did you? Did you gain any experience outside of one environment that would actually allow you to "know better?"

This is an important area of conditioning to consider because there is no fulfillment to be found in following the path of another person or organization, no matter how powerful. There is little honor in living life the way you were told to live without ever asking yourself, "Is this truth I have discovered for myself, or is this a belief I have adopted without much thought, feeling, or experimentation outside of my immediate environment?" Failing to confront the possibility that you would choose to live differently had you not been born into a specific religious organization, or exposed early on to one way of perceiving God, is ultimately failing to walk the most spiritual path available to you; the path that requires you to ask your own questions, receive your own answers, and become our own source of guiding light and unconditional love.

The word religion comes from the Latin word *Religare*, which means "to bind or restrain." The thing that we are often taught to turn to in our most desperate moments, can never actually free us. Religion encourages that you follow and believe in someone else and their experiences. Spirituality is the practice and cultivation of your own relationship with a higher power by placing faith in personal intuition, discernment, and experiences. It is a full surrender to our individual truths, whatever those turn out to be.

"Religion is belief in someone else's experience.
Spirituality is having your own experience."

- Deepak Chopra

"We must here make a clear distinction between belief and faith, because, in general practice, belief has come to mean a state of mind which is almost the opposite of faith. Belief, as I use the word here, is the insistence that the truth is what one would "lief" or wish it to be. The believer will open his mind to the truth on the condition that it fits in with his preconceived ideas and wishes. Faith, on the other hand, is an unreserved opening of the mind to the truth, whatever it may turn out to be. Faith has no preconceptions; it is a plunge into the unknown. Belief clings, but faith lets go. In this sense of the word, faith is the essential virtue of science, and likewise of any religion that is not self-deception."

– Alan Watts

What we are not being taught is that when we place God or any power "out there", outside and beyond ourselves, we can never reach the "atonement," or the heaven that religion promises. Once we realize that there is no saving except for the saving and redemption we create and experience within ourselves, we reach true at-one-ment, which is the enlightenment that follows when we make peace with every aspect of ourselves. Heaven is not a place, but a state of being and is only felt when we are **at-one in this moment.**

Political influence and the media

"Most of the time, we see only what we want to see, or what others tell us to see, instead of really investigating to see what is really there. We embrace illusions only because we are presented with the illusion that they are embraced by the majority. When in truth, they only become popular because they are pounded at us by the media with such an intensity and high level of repetition that its mere force disguises lies and truths. And like obedient schoolchildren, we do not question their validity and swallow everything up like medicine. Why? Because since the earliest days of our youth, we have been conditioned to accept that the direction of the herd, and authority anywhere- is always right."

- Suzy Kassem

Government, religion, education, business and commerce, and the media are all institutions of culture. Law and public policy for most of history have sometimes blatantly but more often subtly, denied women the ability to exercise or express their Wild nature freely. We have been enslaved to cultural norms upheld by a collective agreement to repressive and outdated ways of being.

For instance, underlying the entire abortion debate is the ability of women to exercise and express their sexuality freely without government forcing politics into our bodies. What we need to understand is that the real issue at hand is not whether or not we must all agree on if abortion is right or wrong, but that collectively women must *always* have the right to determine what is best for their bodies, their lives, and their creations. Of course, there is a natural right to life. There is also a natural right to *free-living*, and that is what we still do not have. If together, women would pause long enough to see through this issue, and that what it has created is a battle of women against women; those who would choose to carry every pregnancy to full term versus those who would choose to have the option not to. Making something like this a political debate, that results in policy, and is then enforced by law, traps us all. It traps us in a world where *women specifically* do not have complete power over their own bodies or their own lives. It also creates an illusion of division between women as they unconsciously look down on eachother for not choosing what is "right." Telling someone they cannot choose to abort a pregnancy is as bad as forcing someone to abort a pregnancy. It is the opposite side of the same coin and a fruitless debate. It is not an issue of right or wrong. It is an issue of feminine empowerment. The greatest love you can show another woman (or any person for that matter) is to give her the freedom to make choices you may not necessarily make yourself. Not only does it empower her to continue on her path, it also allows you the freedom and confidence to fully embrace your own. When you are on your own path, you will never be critical of anyone else's. Rather than tie ourselves up in a political discussion, we should be outraged that an issue so intimate and so personally significant was ever allowed to be discussed by men with a larger agenda inside a courtroom.

Issues of this kind are not something that an institution, religious or political, should enforce on a woman's freedom over her own body and life experience. It is the kind of issue that should be nowhere near courtrooms and judges. This is a blatant example of institutional suppression and is a result of thousands of years of patriarchal and religious tradition that has crept into our politics because culture does not compartmentalize. It bleeds over. All conditioning forces affect one another. Religion affects politics, politics affect the media, the media affects education, education affects business and business now affects how free we are to decide what is right for us and our bodies in each moment. All of these institutions of culture sustain one another, they do not sustain freedom of personal expression.

A more subtle example, although just as insidious, would be how women are relegated to lower positions in the workforce and are undervalued by not receiving equal pay for equal work. This is a roll-over from the days when women were, by tradition, expected to stay at home while men conducted all aspects of business. While this paradigm no longer exists in most of the Western world, the unspoken narrative from this historical pattern still favors men.

Women have to be in a position to affect laws and policies in our culture in order to change it. We can't wait for the men to do it. We've been waiting thousands of years for men to do it. People do not generally give up power unless they are forced to.

"Women of the thinking society are the builders of nations. Women of the sentient society are the builders of the world. And given the same honor and dignity as men, women can build a much better and more harmonious world. Harmony and conflict-solving run in their veins. Whereas men have evolved into more authoritarian creatures."

— Abhijit Naskar,

THE BENGAL TIGRESS:
A TREATISE ON GENDER EQUALITY

When women decide to change something, it changes. This is both the blessing and the problem. The power has always been ours, but we have yet to fully claim it. The irony in our predicament is that we have always had the power to change our situation, but instead we have accepted it. These institutions cannot exist as they are if women reject the status quo.

"I am a scientist who studies the human mind, including the sexual differences in mental faculties. The female brain itself is a highly intuitive emotion-processing machine... and I am telling you, ten female thinkers can teach humanity lessons equivalent to the teachings of a hundred male thinkers of history."

— Abhijit Naskar,

THE BENGAL TIGRESS:
A TREATISE ON GENDER EQUALITY

Women would win every single election if they acted together. Religions would not exist if women walked out. Schools would not function, businesses would not thrive, and the media would fall on deaf ears if women decided to act in their own power rather than continue to accept things as they are. As soon as we take responsibility for the world that we have consented to, things will change.

"We have the money, the power, the medical understanding, the scientific know-how, the love and the community to produce a kind of human paradise. But we are led by the least among us – the least intelligent, the least noble, the least visionary. We are led by the least among us and we do not fight back against the dehumanizing values that are handed down as control icons."

–Terence McKenna

Racial and national customs

Unfortunately, most women in the world still labor under adverse suppression. While some progress is being made throughout the world, there are only a few places that have started actively working towards balancing masculine and feminine power. Most of the world, including large parts of Asia, the Middle East, Africa, Latin America, and to a large extent, portions of North America still experience varying degrees of blatant and brutal gender inequality and suppression.

In the Middle East women are punished disproportionately to men. If a woman expresses sexual desire and freedom outside of the narrow confines of their national tradition, she will be killed. The standing of women in Iraq has been deeply affected by war and violence. According to a report from U.N. Women in 2019, the country intensely discriminates against its women and ignores the demand for gender equality through abiding by severely outdated laws and practices. Violence against women is common and "the gender gap is widening with incidents of gender-based violence and limited participation of women and girls in significant fields."

In 2014 Egypt was reported to have the largest number of women and girls who have undergone female genital mutilation. A survey conducted by the Ministry of Health and Population found that this was practiced on 90% of married Egyptian women between ages 15 and 49.

In northern China and India, male children receive preferential treatment and it is common for pregnancies to be aborted once it is determined the sex is female, creating a young population that is disproportionately male (Hannah Richie, Our World Data: Gender Ratio).

In Saudi Arabia, the strictest interpretations of Sharia Law are still practiced today and are enforced by the nation's grossly religious police force. Women are considered minors under male guardians and are not permitted to leave home without them. Though the historic 2015 election granted Saudi women the right to vote for the first time in this nation's history, they are still not permitted to drive and most public spaces are segregated by gender (Martin, R. & Peñaloza, M., NPR).

An Israeli woman needs her husband's permission to get a divorce and a Nigerian husband is permitted to hit his wife, under Section 55 of the Penal Code, for the purposes of "correcting" her (Women and the Law in Nigeria: A Reappraisal).

Guatemala, one of the world's poorest countries, is ranked as one of the worst places to live as a female. An article on Mayan Families states, "A ghastly, unbridled streak of murders left more than 700 women dead last year, for no other reason than because they were female. Of those 700 murdered, less than 2 percent of killers have been brought to justice. For those cases that did make it to court, 90 percent of defendants were acquitted." (Zara Ahmad University at Albany).

Russia's gender-equality legislation that prohibits discrimination on the basis of sex, has been pending for over 13 years (State Duma of the Federal Assembly of the Russian Federation)

There are 32 countries where women need their husband's permission to apply for a passport.

This means in 30 countries, women can't choose for

themselves where they'd like to live. (Women, Business and the Law 2016).

Even in the U.S., the land of the free and home of the brave, "no" doesn't mean "no." In North Carolina. It is not considered rape if a woman withdraws her consent once sexual activity begins. There is a proposed bill to change the law and it is currently being stalled (Molly Redden, The Guardian 2017).

The reason I list so many examples of places where women are suppressed not only by cultural conditioning but by the harmful laws and national customs that are upheld as a result of generations of this conditioning, is so that we can pause to realize that in *most* places around the world, women are not free to live the lives they desire or deserve. Not only have women been subjected to the dominance of men, they are specifically prohibited from expressing their Wild sexuality in ways that ultimately cripple both sexes. The abuser is just as damaged as the abused.

This section was difficult to write because it is so dark and messy. It is also impossible to capture the reality or severity of these women's experiences around the world, our world. I found it challenging to highlight the experiences of other women that reach a level of violence I have never personally known. Though it is unfair to assume that all cultures oppress women, we cannot continue to ignore that the behavioral patterns towards women on a global scale affect us all in a detrimental way. Whether it is the woman who is forced to marry against her will in the name of religion, the woman who was brutally tortured and mutilated for having sex outside of marriage, or the woman who is expected to put up with sexual harassment at work, because "that is just the way it is," **her story is our story**. Her experience is our experience. Her suppression is our suppression. If it is happening to her, it is happening to all of us. We are not separate.

The treatment of women is ultimately a reflection of how we treat life on Earth as a whole. There is no room for the argument of "national heritage" in this discussion any longer. Women make up half of the world's population and have yet to receive half of the respect or influential power. Our entrance into this world depends on a woman and her body. We have yet to honor this truth. Your personal work of shedding the limits and rejecting the boundaries placed on you by any conditioning or controlling force of influence, not only sets you free on a personal level, it demands and instigates change on a massive scale. Though we may not be directly affected in such a negative way, it is important to understand how the view and treatment of women around the world collectively impacts every single one of us.

In cultures where women are the most suppressed, we see the most violence, conflict, turmoil, and abuse. In countries where the balance of masculine and feminine power is restored and respected is where we see the most harmony, advancement, enlightenment, and peace. There is a reason for this. The role of the masculine is to protect and support the feminine, not to control or exploit it. When this happens, the entire world is thrown out of balance, resulting in levels of extreme violence that should never be a part of anyone's experience.

"All the bloodsheds in human history have been caused by men, not women."

-Abhijit Naskar,

THE BENGAL TIGRESS:
A TREATISE ON GENDER EQUALITY

No matter where we live, we must realize how these varying levels of suppression affect our individual psyche and consciousness. It embeds enormous amounts of fear and instills a subconscious belief that we as women cannot live on our own terms. The treatment of women is a clear indication of where we stand as an entire human race.

The point of this section is to shock you out of complacency. This is real. It is happening, and it is happening in our world. Those who are in a position to change, must. The first step toward change is awareness. Once we become aware of the reality of how most women are living around the world, it is our obligation to raise our voices and demand change. The way we start this change is by freeing ourselves from our own conditioning so that we may begin to live and express ourselves in a way that creates balance in this world. Do not underestimate your ability to spark change. If every woman in more enlightened parts of the world, where feminine power is being restored were to embody this change, they would provide an irresistible beacon of light, hope, and courage that the rest of the world cannot help but follow.

Family Expectations

We are far more likely to repeat habits and patterns that are passed down family lines than we are to break them. It is the environment in which we are most susceptible to behave and show up a certain way because of the attachment to "the way we do things." It is easiest around our families to behave passively and become complacent in our authentic expression. It is also the place we learn most of our conditioning albeit religious, political, or social.

This is not to diminish the importance of family and the relationships within our families, as they do provide a sense of familiarity, comfort, and belonging. However, it is important to be aware of how the expectations of our family members, immediate and extended, affect our ability and our willingness to show up as authentic individuals. Especially when we deviate from the norm. It is not uncommon to shy away from things we would otherwise love to do or be simply because of how our family might respond.

When we change or evolve in significant ways, it is not unusual to receive negative feedback from members of our immediate and extended family. Over time, the closest people to us develop an idea about "who we are." When we challenge or change that, we are often met with resistance.

Though we are certainly a part of a family, we are still individual, self-governing souls. It is important to understand that choosing to live differently than your family is not disrespectful, it is necessary for your own evolution and progression. It is also the greatest example you can set for the people you love most.

Peer beliefs and values

Our peers have arguably the greatest influence over us and our lives. At any stage in life (but especially during our most developmental years), they strongly determine our beliefs, attitudes, preferences, and even our desires. They influence the way we speak, the way we dress, the way we respond to certain situations, and ultimately who we are whether we are with them or without them. It matters a great deal who we choose to associate with and who we allow to become our friends. Our friendships are often our most intimate relationships. These are people we care about and their opinions matter, even when they shouldn't. Our need for acceptance compels us to think and behave in certain ways around our friends and peer groups.

Our peers are the closest part of our cultural experience. Their conditioning directly influences and becomes a part of our own conditioning. When I use the term, "conditioned" I mean unconscious behavior, things we do without even thinking. It is important that we all examine what we are doing in relation to what our peers are doing. Are we saying certain things only because they do? Would we speak differently if they were not present? Do we act differently when we are with them compared to when we are alone? Are we putting on a show?

If this is happening even on a small scale, it is a good idea to create some distance in these relationships until you can fully realize that you are not here to impress people, you are here to love them, and you can only love them if you are able to show up in full authenticity.

Cultural conditioning exists in nearly every area of our lives and often keeps us from forming deep, meaningful, and lasting connections because it keeps us from acting in our true authenticity. Authentic connection is the only connection. Anything else is an illusion. I hope you will challenge yourself to remove cultural (i.e. familial, religious, social, political) limits and barriers and see what you are left with. Remember, you can pick it all back up again if you decide it serves you, but you will never know until you feel what it is like to think and live without it.

FIRE

Wild child, gypsy soul
Take off the mask and drop the role
Run like the wind, burn hot as coal
You were not made to be controlled.

—Indigo

The first step to living a life free from the influence of old, conditioned patterns is to identify where this conditioning exists in your life and how it affects your thoughts, feelings, and behavior. With this new awareness, you will start to notice the ways it impacts important aspects of your life and your authentic expression. It is important to see how conditioning can, and likely has shaped your entire belief system and life experience.

We have been mesmerized by the promises of the old ways of doing things. We hang on to old patterns and stories with the hope that just maybe, if we cling to them a little longer, we will experience the fairytale ending. We operate under the false belief that perhaps the problem is us, not the story, and that by committing ourselves to it, we too will be saved like every other princess. In doing so we repeat destructive patterns and wonder what we have done to deserve a different outcome than what was promised. This happens always and only when we spin the wheel of a broken story, void of truth, and allow ourselves to be the gears of a system we would never actually create ourselves. The danger is not in being told the story, but believing and romanticizing what we have been told rather than continuing to lean into our own intuition, no matter how lovely the fairytales we once believed seem to be.

In our modern world, there are countless forces that oppose our Wild natural state. Rather than fearing or resisting this, understand that these opposing and sometimes debilitating forces must exist in order for you to learn to fully determine and embrace who you are. They must exist in order for you to choose a different life; a life dedicated to the reclamation of feminine empowerment and freedom.

If you remain in ignorance of these forces or in anger towards them, you become the easiest target of their undoing. All that is required to overcome and move beyond their reach is the acknowledgment of their existence as part of what *is*. The allowance of these forces without the acceptance of their power over you is what enables you to transcend their trap and live a life above their influence.

As long as we believe that the power is in a cultural, religious, or societal idea and not within ourselves, within our feminine nature, we will be killed off and lost to the churning wheels of outdated societal rules and patterns. It is time to shift from living falsely to living freely.

When we succumb to being the "nice girl", the "sweet thing", "lady-like" and "proper", believing in the promise that we will then receive security, eternal love, the excitement of adventure, or even hot sex, we give up the instinctual part of ourselves that would instead naturally be bigger, bolder, faster, louder, wilder, and independent- not needing or requiring fulfillment through a fairytale.

"When a woman is exhorted to be compliant, cooperative, and quiet, to not make upset or go against the old guard, she is pressed into living a most unnatural life- a life that is self-blinding... without innovation. The worldwide issue for women is that under such conditions they are not only silenced, they are put to sleep. Their concerns, their viewpoints, their own truths are vaporized."

— Clarissa Pinkola Estes

It is not only our nature, but our innate power as women to see more than what is visible, to hear both the said and unsaid, and to sense beyond what is offered as "possible." If there is something that is off-limits, prohibited, or forbidden, it is our duty to look there, to shed light on that dark place, and determine for ourselves whether or not it deserves to be hidden, locked away, and left untouched. Our ability to uncover what has been hidden, to gather what has been scattered, and to remember what has been lost, enables us to return to the deepest parts of ourselves, our truth, and our nature. These are the parts of women and the Wild feminine that nurture and honor all of life by finding and releasing the places that can and must expand.

The most important questions you can ask are;

What here is not seen but felt?

What else is true?

What do I hear that is not being said?

What do I know deep within that I wish I could ignore?

What inside me have I left to die because "wild animals" aren't allowed inside?

We are born in love. Fear, we learn. Returning to the Wild is the process of unlearning fear, prejudices, limitations, and expectations about what it means to be a woman so we can fully accept love back into our lives. It is time to get out of your own way and break free from everything you were taught so you can return to what you know.

We cannot wake up an unconscious culture by screaming out that it is asleep. We can only awaken ourselves to deeper truths and begin to live in alignment with what we find and feel to be Wild, natural, and real. Personal awareness is the most powerful way to undo conditioning.

You are an independent, sovereign soul, which means by nature, you are independent and self-governing. When you are not your true self, a powerful, expressive, free, and Wild Woman, the world suffers as much as you do. It loses a crucial piece of the whole.

Seybrielle's Story

When I think back on what set me free from social and cultural limitations, being married to a woman before it was legal in Utah was a big step in abandoning my conditioning around sexuality. Specifically, my journey back to my most natural self came through heartbreak, having to go through a divorce that I didn't want to go through, having to let go of the life that I thought I really wanted so that I could discover my true nature. For most of us, the path appears when everything else begins to fall away, what I thought was real and what would last forever began to crumble. My outside world started to change, leading me deep within myself has meant facing a lot of pain and grief of the old ways that can no longer remain on this return home.

This relationship along with its demise led me to the most freeing experience of my life which was moving to Costa Rica. The wild untamed spirit of nature unraveled me. I was brought back into a remembrance that we are one and the same. This path was not paved and I most certainly didn't feel guided or led but more like a complete free fall into the unknown. Until I could finally let myself be free for no one else but me. My most natural wild self has been an initiation of sorts into the power of what it means to be one with nature and continuous cultivation of not allowing myself to get completely swept away by the ways of the world while simultaneously learning to walk in this place with my heart wide open. Allowing myself to live a life defined by nature's tides and rhythms and tuning into my own cycles. Living in the land of Pura Vida created a space for me to realize that my worth was not in what I could do or have, it wasn't about being productive it was about being present and having the ability to go with the flow. In making this move it required me to relinquish and sale all of my material belongings and go move in with my father which set into motion a perfect arena for me to look at my own judgments about the circumstances I was creating for myself to learn from and taught me a lot about the outside pressures and expectations I had previously placed on myself and others. To just BE in a new place that no one knew me, gave me the freedom to be who I was in that moment, no need to impress or keep up with my old story and social conditioning of what success looked like and to be worthy to enjoy life.

Honoring my soul's path, and freeing myself from all previous expectations has allowed me to feel alive, I feel life, there's a connection to myself and the world around me that no amount of words could even begin to describe. I don't have children, but the reverence I have for my own life feels like the love of a mother who just gave birth to her child, I feel that for my own life and I cherish myself and all of life as a precious gift. That feeling of looking out into a sunset and feeling so connected to the beauty of life and being able to have moments of just awestruck wonderment of just what a gift it is to be at home wherever I go, with whoever I meet, there is no more seeking outside myself for some missing piece, I AM it. Life just IS and what a beautiful masterpiece it is. When the seemingly impossible becomes possible through acts of love, forgiveness, and healing. The coming together that has happened since this homecoming blows my mind and implodes my heart.

My wish is that as women, we will continue to help each other see the truth. Simply put, I hope that open, honest communication can begin to take place between us so we can honor each other's feelings and authentic expression. It is important to realize that most of us likely want the same things, but our fear and the avoidance of our pain keeps us silent and separated. I hope that our love and desire to relate to one another can reveal itself so we can enjoy our lives before the pain of death forces us to remember what really matters.

Your own love is the greatest love you will ever know and it is only through loving and honoring your own life that it will grow. Your love is a gift that could never possibly be reimbursed, so give it freely without expectations, it will always come back to you from unlikely places. So be sure to let it in, to be open to receive and know that you do not have to do anything to be worthy, you already are. For what you give, you shall always receive but it doesn't always happen immediately. A love that lasts a lifetime, takes time, so take care of yourself, take care of your heart, take care of your life and every person you meet, see them as a part of yourself that just wants to be held, so love without limits, discover compassion through your own suffering and the suffering of others. Your love has the power to heal all wounds, mend all separation. Your love is why you came here so don't hold back, let it all in. because when this is all said and done you'll have to let it all go, so feel it all, fill it all, every place, every space.

Your purpose and path unfolds as you awaken your senses, remember what feels good to you, what makes you feel alive. You are your purpose, your path is just you, simply living a life that you love, it doesn't need to look like anything. It's not your job title or what you do but how it is that you share yourself in any situation. On your path, just love, be kind, listen and learn. Stop looking for it outside of yourself, everything you need to know about how to live your life can be found inside. Meditate, pray, sit in nature, meet new people, expand your perception, serve and give back to those who could use your love, time and attention. Your presence is your purpose so give the gift of you to the world by loving all of yourself.

Seybrielle Daniels

Medicine Woman
SEYBRIELLE@GMAIL.COM

Autobiography of Eve

Wearing nothing but snakeskin
boots, I blazed a footpath, the first
radical road out of that old kingdom
toward a new unknown.
When I came to those great flaming gates
of burning gold,
I stood alone in terror at the threshold
between Paradise and Earth.
There I heard a mysterious echo:
my own voice
singing to me from across the forbidden
side. I shook awake—
at once alive in a blaze of green fire.
Let it be known: I did not fall from grace.
I leapt
to freedom..

— Ansel Elkins

SHEDDING
SKIN

WORK ON PAPER

What a shame it is that we still accept the archaic myth of the fall of man by Woman. Surely She is not his fall but his rise, not his shame but his hope, not his defeat but his truth.

Women, shed the old stories and be who you came here to be.

—Indigo

For most people, overcoming limiting beliefs and shedding cultural conditioning is a daunting proposition. Thought patterns and beliefs that are deeply ingrained from early childhood on, make this change overwhelming, uncomfortable, even terrifying. It is okay to feel this way. In fact, recognizing that you are being limited by this fear will motivate you to rebel against what limits your life so you can regain true independence.

To ensure you feel confident in this process, I have written a simple step-by-step guide for how to shed this old skin and rid yourself of beliefs and patterns you may have unknowingly established as a result of social and environmental conditioning. In the next few pages, we will review simple steps you can take to shed these layers of conditioning, no matter where they came from, so you can recover and embrace your Wild self and innate power. Deep conditioning acts as an invisible, restrictive skin. You can only move as much as it allows. Let's shed what does not serve us. The only limits that exist are the ones that we consent to.

Step 1: Make the decision.

Every woman's journey back to the Wild self begins with making the decision to live differently. In some cases, it may feel like a leap of faith or an act of sincere hope. All you need to do is make the decision to begin because the power of that decision is half the battle. This is the decision to love yourself fully by removing all fear and shame-based conditioning programmed into you by culture without your consent, so you can experience limitless joy, pleasure, and freedom as your Wild, authentic self. Isn't that what you really want? Then decide now.

Step 2: Identify limiting beliefs.

The easiest way to do this is to sit down with a pen and paper and write down any beliefs you have about yourself and this life that you feel limit you in some way. I will often include any belief that comes up, even if it doesn't seem to limit me. I am surprised by how often beliefs that seem "good," still limit my experience and expression.

Begin by asking, "what are the "rules" that drive my

behavior with fear and shame?" When you write these things down and really look at what little validity they have, you begin to take conscious control of them. You begin to take responsibility for your conditioning, and you begin to realize that it is something you have the power to change or discard altogether. By doing so, you regain power over your life. Here are a few examples of what conditioned thoughts and beliefs can look like;

1. I am selfish if I care for myself first.

2. I am not supposed to ask for help or support. Especially over little things.

3. God is taking note of all my mistakes and will punish me later.

4. I have to work hard to get anything in life.

5. What other people think about me matters. A lot.

6. If I am true to myself, I will end up alone.

7. There is simply not enough to go around. Everything is a competition.

8. I have to look a certain way to be desired.

9. If I don't go to college, I'll never be successful.

10. My role in my relationship has to look a certain way or it won't work.

11. God will damn me if I enjoy sex the way I want to.

12. My parents will be disappointed or ashamed of me if I dress sexy.

13. People will think I'm a slut if I have a lot of sex.

14. If I pleasure myself, I am abusing my body.

15. I can't have sex outside of marriage. It's a sin.

16. Sex can only be between a man and a woman.

17. Sex can only happen with two people. Never more.

18. My body should always be covered. Nudity is bad.

To ensure you stay present in this process as you read, I have provided journal pages below where you can start your own list.

My limiting beliefs are...

My limited beliefs are...

After writing each one down, ask yourself, "Is this really true?" I know you will be surprised to find that most often, any belief that limits your life, has never been your truth it.

Step 3: Take control of your conditioning.

Realize that all of the beliefs you have are just that, beliefs. They are not necessarily true or even rational and are thought patterns that exist and repeat in your mind. They can be changed, or in many cases discarded altogether. You can make the choice at any time to re-evaluate and rewrite your beliefs. Rewriting beliefs is how you shed the tight skin of your conditioning. Look back at your list. Check to see how many of your beliefs are based on your own personal experience and how many are things you have simply accepted from other people, places, or things as "the norm." How many of them are based on fear or shame rather than love? How many are designed to limit your ability to experience joy and pleasure? How many of them keep you "checking boxes" to get into heaven? How many of them simply make you feel awful? Think about what it would be like to discard anything that does not bring your life more love, pleasure, and fulfillment.

Isn't it liberating that you have the power to decide what is true for you personally? Would your life be simpler? More fulfilling? Happier? If so, change or discard whatever is necessary. Take conscious control. Rewrite each statement to affirm what you want for yourself, not what others have shamed or scared you into believing. Only you know what is true for you, and only you can decide what is best for your life and happiness. Let your Wild self reign free.

I am changing my beliefs to...

I am changing my beliefs to...

I am changing my beliefs to...

Once you have reframed your beliefs, review them again. You may find you are still limiting yourself based on other people's desires and expectations. Continue the exercise until the page bleeds raw with your individual truth. Imagine living by that code. Imagine living free from fear and shame. Welcome to the Wild. Welcome home.

"Waking up to who you are requires letting go of who you imagine yourself to be."

— Alan Watts

Step 4: Explore and experiment.

Truth and knowledge can only be gained through personal experience. Returning to your Wild, natural self demands that you place your attention and faith in your own experiences rather than using the experience and opinions of others as a crutch. The best way to either solidify or discard a belief is to challenge it. See for yourself if it is valid or not by paying attention to how it personally affects your own feelings, intuition, and of course life experiences. Many of the religious teachings I was exposed to as a child, turned out to be completely untrue in my own experience. Once I realized this, it became very easy for me to shed.

If you adopt a philosophy and habit of exploration and experimentation, you will quickly begin to see for yourself which beliefs assist you on your path and which ones hinder your personal progression. Once you let go of the fear and shame you learned to feel as a child, as an adolescent, or even as an adult you can start asking, "What is my actual experience?" "Does it feel good?" "Do I enjoy this?" "Do I want this?" Imagine there are no outside influences to dictate or determine what is right or wrong, or how something should or should not feel. Feel it for yourself. That is how you find the truth, your truth. This is the only truth that matters. When you fully realize that you can trust yourself, your body, and your feelings, you are free.

Step 5: Embrace pleasure.

It is crazy that I have to say this, but pleasure is GOOD. Experiences that bring you true pleasure are good to create, explore, and recreate. Our culture has conditioned us to go to war against our own natural desires and instincts, especially in regard to limiting or abstaining from the pleasures of our physical bodies. Leaning into and embracing the pleasure of your body brings you back to your center. Your body cannot lie. It doesn't know how to lie. The more we open ourselves to physical pleasure, the more sensitive we become in our capacity to feel everything in life. It is the gateway to connecting with your intuition, your more subtle senses, and your ability to determine what is true and untrue for you in your life.

"Originally and naturally, sexual pleasure was the good, the beautiful, the happy, that which united human with nature in general. When sexual feelings and religious feelings became separated from one another, that which is sexual was forced to become the bad, the internal, the diabolical."

– Wilhelm Reich

The false idea that pleasure, especially sexual pleasure, is somehow evil, is at the root of our unhappiness and is the seed of many of our most serious problems. This does not mean that pleasure should be sought at the expense of health or the welfare of others. But where these factors are not an issue, it is natural to seek to maximize our pleasure (this should be obvious, and shows just how bizarre our cultural norm has become).

Of course, one of the greatest pleasures we can experience

as women is erotic sexual pleasure. If you don't believe me for some reason, I refer you to step four. Challenge me. As soon as you let go of self-judgment, fear, and shame, accepting and seeking pleasure becomes the most natural and wonderful, self-loving, life-affirming thing in this world. It deserves to be the obvious path.

Step 6: Find your tribe.

Perhaps the most difficult obstacle in seeking to overcome limiting beliefs and enjoying unlimited feminine power and pleasure, are your existing relationships (parents, siblings, friends, teachers, leaders, etc.) who are part of the cultural web that keeps us limited by the fear and shame of old traditions. There is another important choice you must make no matter how much these people love you and no matter how much you love them; are they in control of your life, or are you? If you are surrounded by people whose influence keeps you bound in the cultural cocoon, it is time to break free and create new boundaries. This does not have to happen all at once (although that is an option). It is time to form new relationships with people who share your desire to be free, and who will support and encourage you in your transformation. It will be easier than you think. Remember, what you seek is seeking you.

As you begin to form these new relationships, it will become easier to let go of the old, limiting relationships, or at least no longer allow them to have primary influence over you and your life. As you discover that there are many wonderful men and women who are embracing a similar path of freedom and feminine power, you will feel a new sense of empowerment yourself.

Step 7: Say YES to your Wild sexuality.

Rather than continuing to suppress or ignore your natural desires and yearning for sexual pleasure and fulfillment, start saying "yes!" inspired by your newfound enthusiasm, instead of "no" out of obligation influenced by the fear and shame that was never yours to carry. You will discover your true capacity for enjoyment as a woman through your body and your strengthened connection with your Wild self.

Enter a new world of experiences by exploring new ways to speak, dress, and move that make you feel sexy and alive.

Step 8: Make a list.

Shedding limitations is like getting into shape, you need a plan of how to get you there over time. While some are able to plunge in all at once, most of us find it easier to wade in a bit more cautiously, taking time to get acclimated with each step as we go deeper. Whatever pace you choose, continue to challenge your limitations, push your boundaries (cultural comfort zones) and violate "taboos" until you are free. As you do, celebrate each new experience as a victory of self-love and empowerment over cultural suppression, fear, and shame.

The best way to do this is to make a list (without any of your previous judgment, fear, or shame interfering) of all the Wild, erotic, sexy, or controversial things you have ever thought of, wondered about, or wished you could try (even the things that seem completely taboo). For me, this started with small things like piercing my nose or my nipple and wearing clothing that highlighted my favorite parts of my body. I experimented with plant medicines and started posing nude for my friend's cameras. Later, I progressed to things like having sex outside of a committed relationship, having sex with women, and having sex with multiple people at the same time. I took conscious control of my own life. Not only was it fun, it freed me to be exactly who I wanted to be all while teaching me how to create my own healthy boundaries.

Let your imagination run wild. Set your inner desires free. This is not encouragement to participate in reckless or dangerous activities (your most Wild, natural self would never direct you towards that). It is, however, an invitation to find your edge and move beyond it. There is so much there for you to find and learn about your true self. Think of this list as your personal empowerment "training program." I suggest starting with simpler things like I did. This helps you expand your range and capacity for processing your experiences. The last thing you want to do is start with something so big that it scares you back into the same shame you started with. Be kind to yourself. Move slowly and remain present. Notice how you feel in every moment and follow those feelings. Pay attention to what makes you feel alive.

You will be surprised by how much joy, fun, excitement, and pleasure this can bring into your life. It will also help you identify where and when you choose to do or not do things based on other people's opinions of you. Acknowledge it, and let it go. It is time to adopt a new way of living. When you push yourself to your edge and challenge yourself to try things that you normally never would, you will discover a whole new level of confidence, power, charisma, and creativity you had no idea you possessed. This practice literally cracks the cocoon.

Here is an example of a list to get you started. Feel free to add, subtract, and adjust as you feel. Not all change has to be hard. This gets to be fun.

1. Wear an outfit that makes you feel sexy. Go out. Show yourself off.

2. Dance naked in front of a mirror.

3. Sit in front of a mirror and look at your vulva for 10 minutes. Time yourself, then write down everything you notice and love about her. *Learn the difference between the words vulva and vagina. Get to know your own body.

4. Touch your own body.

5. Try a new sex position.

6. Hike up a mountain and sunbathe naked in private.

7. Walk around your house naked. *Note: do these things until you feel uncomfortable. Then ask, what made me feel like I needed to stop?

8. Model lingerie for your partner.

9. Take nude photos with a trusted friend. Let her pick her favorites, then you pick yours. Share your favorite parts of each other's bodies.

10. Go to a strip club. Get a dance, then dance with him/her.

11. Skip the undies.

12. Get the piercing you've always wanted.

13. Go on a nature walk (naked of course).

14. Kiss a woman (or a man if you normally don't).

15. Let a man go down on you until you orgasm.

16. Let a woman go down on you until you orgasm.

17. Have a topless dance party with your best friends.

18. Get a vibrator.

19. Wear a tiny bikini to the beach ("But nip slips!" Exactly).

20. Again, TOUCH YOUR OWN BODY.

Of course, your list will include anything else you can dream up. The whole point is to prove to yourself that your beliefs surrounding your sexuality and sensuality are largely fabricated by social and cultural forces. Challenge your limits and see what conditioned inhibitions can be overcome. See if you can disregard all of it, and start to feel into things yourself. If you can do it with sex and sexuality, you can do it with anything. I encourage you to use your imagination and push your boundaries until you are completely fearless; until you are free. Surrender to your Wild and embrace the pure untainted enjoyment of your erotic pleasure. You will discover a power you never imagined you possessed. That is your Wild Woman.

Step 9: Channel your erotic power.

As you move forward gaining confidence and discovering your true feminine power, you can channel it in many creative ways to fulfill whatever purpose, goal, or intention you may have. You will develop radiant sexual energy (charisma) that others will find irresistible. You will begin to realize that this energy can be channeled into accomplishing short and long term goals. Erotic energy has always been the heart of feminine power. By learning to harness and direct it, you literally become a Goddess worthy of worship (the word worship means "to serve" or "to work for") and the world will bend to your will and desires. Patriarchal culture has attempted, and to a large degree succeeded, to suppress this power, going so far as to burn women at the stake as "witches" for using it. Pause here for a moment with me and see this clearly. Feel this deeply; they were not witches, they were women. Mothers, daughters, sisters, friends, healers, lovers, and seers. These women were physical manifestations of truth, the same as you and I.

It is time we each take back this power to usher in a new age of Wild feminine embodiment.

"We are the granddaughters of the [WOMEN]
they weren't able to burn."

– Tish Thawer

Step 10: Become a mentor.

It is true that you cannot claim mastery of a thing until you can teach it to another. As your Wild power begins to mature, you will likely feel the desire to support those who are only just beginning to learn, and those who have yet to awaken to who and what they really are. I speak from experience when I say that you will find so much joy and fulfillment in teaching and helping other women, especially younger women, who seem to be eager for this natural and authentic way of life. They feel the call of the Wild. Lead them.

---

*"Lead by example. Support women on their way...
trust that they will extend a hand to those who
follow."*

— Mariela Dabbah

This ten-step guide for overcoming limiting beliefs and conditioning focuses on sexual conditioning for an important reason. Our sexual nature is the primary aspect of divine feminine power that has been suppressed, throwing virtually every other aspect of life out of balance. By unlocking and allowing your feminine sexuality to emerge and blossom, an enormous amount of confidence and power will become available to you that can be applied in all aspects of your life.

Breaking free from the cocoon of cultural conditioning will allow the butterfly (your Wild self) to emerge and take wing. The butterfly is nature's most beautiful and powerful symbol of the process of transformation and awakening, which is a metaphor for the evolution of the soul as it emerges into new magnificent forms. Like the caterpillar, we come to a point in our progress where we feel the need to change. Our life is no longer fulfilling, and we sense that we are capable of something far greater. Just like the little caterpillar, we realize we must let go of our current understanding and limitations in order to embrace a higher form of existence. The old form must dissolve so the new form can emerge.

─◦◦✶◦◦─

"Transformation literally means going beyond your form."

-Wayne Dyer

Metaphors for this process are found abundantly throughout all of nature. Cynthia Occelia points out that, "for a seed to achieve its greatest expression, it must come completely undone. The shell cracks, its insides come out and everything changes. To someone who doesn't understand growth, it would look like complete destruction." This process is simple, but simple does not always mean easy. It will bring you to your edge over and over and over again. It will cause old, unhealed, and unprocessed wounds to resurface. It will require you to face them and to free them. Shedding skin is messy. It is a destructive process as it forces you to detach from ideas, beliefs, patterns, behaviors, desires, and stories that you have falsely identified with for your entire life. It is also a creative process because it allows you to emerge as exactly who and what you want to be.

This is how you take conscious control of who you are,

what you believe, and what you want to experience in your life. Real change means giving up one reality for another. It means dissolving everything you were taught to be so you can emerge, embody, and embrace who and what you really are. I invite you to emerge from your cocoon. Come fly with me.

"Your new life is going to cost you your old one. It's going to cost you your comfort zone and your sense of direction. It's going to cost you relationships and friends. It's going to cost you being liked, and understood. But that doesn't matter. Because the people who are meant for you are going to meet you on the other side. And you're going to build a new comfort zone around the things that actually move you forward. And instead of liked, you're going to be loved. Instead of understood, you're going to be seen. All you're going to lose is what was built for a person you no longer are. Let it go."

—Brianna Wiest

Don't stop all that's coming
Lean in
It will feel like a flood gate
Begin
Please let down your mind
There is more you will find
But you have to first choose to release it
To shed it
To leave it
To free it
You have to be willing to die
To let it All open your mind
Leave the world that you know far behind
Then remember this rhyme
Because in it you'll find
All that is needed to reap it
To know it
To grow it
To keep it
Have you been willing to meet yourself?

To match yourself
Hear yourself
See yourself
You say you just want to Be Yourself!
But you stop yourself
Small yourself
Beat yourself
You will never get through it All
If you won't Be it All
Match it All
Hear it All
Hold it All
How will you ever obtain it All?
If you stop it All
Small it All
Smash it All
Box it All
Have you not paused to remember
YOU ARE THE ALL
You've said that you want to come See yourself.
Then you evade yourself
Scathe yourself
Hate yourself
What are these things you take as yourself?
Drop yourself
Let yourself
Know yourself

Only then are you able to feel yourself
To match yourself
Hold yourself
Heal yourself
When you are the All then you'll See yourself
Have yourself
Know yourself
Be yourself

—Indigo

A LESSON FROM PSILOCYBIN

EXHUMING
BONES

Bones create a framework for your physical body. They provide the structure for everything layered on top. This is a perfect metaphor as we continue to explore what it means to shed old layers in order to uncover the deeper parts of your true self. Your bones are your center and your center remains untouched by cultural and environmental influences. This is where the real you exists. The way we access our center is by unveiling the parts of ourselves that have been hidden, suppressed, restrained, censored, and concealed for any reason. I like to call this part of the process, exhuming bones. Like an archaeologist gently digging to uncover old dinosaur bones that reveal the truth of times past, we will dive deep into our inner worlds to uncover the truth of who we have always been.

"The body remembers, the bones remember, the joints remember, even the little finger remembers."

—Clarissa Pinkola Estes

WOMEN WHO RUN WITH THE WOLVES

Within us, there are soul bones of the Wild self. The parts of us that cannot be destroyed only buried and forgotten. In archetypal symbology, bones represent the indestructible force. When you lay a body into the Earth the only thing that remains no matter how much time passes, are the bones. You are not dissolving yourself entirely. Not everything about you is conditioned, not everything about you is learned. There is a center that has always been there, that has always been real, and that cannot be destroyed.

Though shedding the tight skin of cultural conditioning may feel uncomfortable, it is the only way you can start to recollect or remember your real, natural, and Wild self. Notice the word *remember*. Not only does the word mean to recall what has been lost or forgotten, the word re-member literally means to put back together, to bring back lost and scattered pieces and again make them whole. This is what you are doing in a very real sense. You are re-membering lost and forgotten pieces of your soul that have been buried like bones beneath layers of cultural conditioning, religious ruling, and social pressures.

Ask yourself, what aspects of myself have been buried, and how do I make them come alive again? Like ancient, clean, white, bones, this is the part of you that cannot be affected by conditioning, though they may lay hidden because of it. It is a lot harder to reclaim aspects of yourself and your nature when there are layers upon layers of harsh, false, learned patterns of conditioning that block the path back to your Wild self. This is why we must begin by removing the influence and control of these old limits and patterns. When you become free from these, it is much easier to uncover and see what has been forgotten.

There are also times when life forces this inner work. We have all experienced circumstances that have given us no choice but to shed who we once were, turn inward, and uncover a deeper knowledge, strength, and power than we were previously accessing or leveraging.

Michelle's Story (my sweet mom)

For the first 40 years of my life, I would describe myself as simple, honest, trusting, quiet, and non-confrontational. I always tried to do the right thing and I thought I was doing "all the right things" to ensure I lived a life full of blessings and happiness. I experienced only minor trails and problems and was the picture-perfect Mormon mom, complete with 8 wonderful children.

One afternoon, a 5-minute phone call changed everything on a dime. The person on the other side of the line informed me that my husband had been arrested and was in jail. My mind was swimming as I had no idea what it could possibly be for. In a single moment, my life and the life of my family as we knew it, had changed forever.

Every day for the next couple of years I was slammed

with the most difficult situations I had ever encountered. I was forced far outside my comfort zone and was dealing with a life that was different from anything I ever could have imagined. Most days I did not know how I would make it through to the next. Not only was I facing the shock and repercussions of what my husband's choices, but I was also suddenly forced to figure out in a very short amount of time, how I would keep the family business going to provide the income my family needed by negotiating with business partners on matters I knew nothing about, all while trying to keep myself together enough to support the wellbeing of my children amidst this trauma. My faith was shaken, I didn't know who to trust, I felt embarrassed and ashamed. Our neighbors of nearly 20 years were quiet and distant, judgmental and unkind. Feelings of abandonment and hopelessness set it fast.

I had to let go of who I thought I was, and the life I thought I'd live and look deep inside myself. I discovered a woman I never knew was there. I now know how each and every one of us is capable of digging deep and becoming more than we ever thought we could be. Life is going to hit us hard at one point or another. The only constant thing in our lives is change. We must be ready and willing to adapt, dig deep, and have faith that there is an untapped reservoir of strength inside of our own being. I know that tapping into this is what made me happy and whole as a woman. This will look different for everyone, but what I know for sure is that every woman has this untapped reservoir of strength that will be there for her when she needs it most.

I look at how my 5 beautiful, most incredible daughters handled what was thrown their way, and while they are all so unique in the paths they have chosen and what they love, they each have risen far above this experience learning and growing so much, and are stronger and the better for it. I think of each one of them and that is what I see - a deep strength and assurance in these women who know who they are, and are equipped to handle anything that comes their way.

My message to any woman would simply be this: YOU have the power, the ability to choose how you will act and react when life hits you hard. I say bring it .... doesn't matter how hard it hits you, what matters is how you choose to handle it. Know that you can do it. Know that whatever you may be asked to deal with, you have what it takes to harness that power within you. Find the wild part in you, express it only as you see fit, and be a source of strength for yourself and those around you.

Removing layers of learned beliefs, patterns, and behaviors allow us to follow our own intuitive thoughts and feelings, rather than wander through life confused by thoughts and feelings that have been influenced by our culture and environment. It also allows us to anchor into a deeper level of courage, strength, and confidence than we would ever otherwise gain access to. Our bones are the doorways of the Wild self.

"The doors to the world of the wild Self are few but precious. If you have a deep scar, that is a door, if you have an old, old story, that is a door. If you love the sky and the water so much you almost cannot bear it, that is a door. If you yearn for a deeper life, a full life, a sane life, that is a door."

—Clarissa Pinkola Estes

Dedicate time each day to spend alone, quiet, and in nature. Allow for old memories, feelings, sensations, and desires to arise and resurface. A wilder part of the heart is awakened when we take the time to travel through our inner worlds and place our attention on the tender places we have mostly, if not always ignored. Exhuming bones is soul work. It is the process of honoring and reclaiming every aspect of ourselves that was tamed, discounted, or disregarded by the world.

We must realize that as we uncover and reclaim these aspects of ourselves, at first, we may not like everything we find. This is in large part due to the fact that we have been conditioned to perceive certain things about ourselves as either "good" or "bad." Many of our suppressed feelings and emotions will lead us back to old wounds that were never fully processed or healed. We will be led there to change the story of these past traumas that are controlling present behavior. Now, with our new perspective and understanding of how conditioned beliefs and behaviors affect our lives and the world around us, we can shed light on the confusion, grief, and despair we may have experienced in the past. Exhuming bones leads us back to our full light and power by reacquainting us with shadow. It is important that we give love and attention to these darker parts of ourselves and our lives, remembering that though we may not like everything we find and feel, there is nothing to be afraid of.

It is easy to love our light, but we are not made of light alone. We carry darkness too. It is essential. We can only experience light if it has something to shine on. Our darker aspects, our personal underworlds, and yes, even our deaths (shedding cultural conditioning is a type of death; you are trading one life for another), are what give our light authenticity and meaning. When we learn to love and integrate both aspects of ourselves, we become whole.

We become fearless. We become free.

Our willingness to visit the darker corners of lives, to travel to our own depths and accept whatever we find, teaches us that our fears are baseless and enables us to expand our light. Exhuming bones is the process of shining light into dark, transmuting pain into power, and remembering that Love is all there is. It is how we remember who we were before the world took hold of us.

"Bone by bone, hair by hair, Wild Woman comes back. Through night dreams, through events half understood and half remembered."

— Clarissa Pinkola Estes,

WOMEN WHO RUN WITH THE WOLVES

In our modern society, especially in the Western world, we tend to emphasize, almost to the exclusion of everything else, the material and the rational. These are the things you can touch and see. Although we intuitively know it is there, we exclude and ignore the unseen world, the spiritual, magical, mystical side of the universe. Connection to and trust in the unseen brings us a far more powerful understanding of ourselves and the world around us because it demands that we get out of our heads and return to our hearts. It demands that we be Wild.

Knowledge of how to access, interact with, and utilize the unseen world has been hugely suppressed. Its suppression goes hand-in-hand with the overall suppression of the feminine because the unseen is divinely and innately, feminine. Our intuitive sense and our connection to these mystical, heavenly realms and forces, transcend rationality. It is an important part of our nature and what we refer to as, the Divine Feminine. The Divine Feminine is what connects us to the intelligence of the heart, or collective consciousness. Shedding cultural conditioning and reclaiming the Wild self by exhuming our bones is internal work. It is the first step to building a relationship with the unseen world because it is done by coming into the senses and feeling past what is seen. Our feelings are guides to the doors of the Wild self, which lead us into the spiritual world of the soul. *This* is where true personal connection is made.

Take a moment now to identify and write down anything about yourself you have felt the need to bury, tame, or suppress over the years in order to please, achieve, or fit in with the outside world. What were you like as a child? Are you different now? Did you give something up? What have you parted with? What parts of yourself have you abandoned because a child could be loud, a child could be messy, a child could be naked, a child could be Wild... But a woman? Never.

As a child I was Wild, but now I sometimes...

As a child I was Wild, but now I
sometimes...

As a child I was Wild, but now I
sometimes...

Shedding the skin of the outer self and relinquishing your persona or social mask in order to exhume the soul bones that put you back in touch with your inner Wild self, can be a slow, painful, and challenging process. It is also the most fascinating, fulfilling, and freeing work you will ever do.

"Walk straight ahead for that last hard mile. Go up and knock on the old weathered door. Climb up to the cave. Crawl through the window of a dream. Sift the desert and see what you find. It is the only work we have to do. You wish psychoanalytic advice?

Go gather bones. "

—Clarissa Pinkola Estés

WOMEN WHO RUN WITH THE WOLVES

FLESHING OUT

After you have shed skin and exhumed old soul bones, you may feel raw and exposed. Slowly, and through new, personal experiences, free of the conditioning and suppression that previously weighed you down, you will begin to put flesh back on your bones. You are taking conscious control of your transformation. As you redefine who and what you are, you resurrect your inner Wild Woman. She changes you from the inside- out. This is your rebirth, and with it comes the practice of building and creating your own life. True transformation means transcending your old form.

Free from the weight of the world, you get to determine your experience and reality. The order of this process is critical because only once you have shed suppressive conditioning and re- membered the buried and forgotten parts of yourself, can you uncover your true purpose in this life. Your purpose puts flesh back on the old soul bones giving your life luster and meaning. Committing to your purpose is how you answer the call of the Wild. It is how you welcome the Wild Woman back and allow her to live through you.

"So, let us push on now, and remember ourselves back to the wild soul. Let us sing her flesh back onto our bones."

– Clarissa Pinkola Estes

This part of the process will look different for every one of us because it is completely dependent upon your unique desires and authentic expression. It is critical that you stay in tune with your intuition and personal truth. Be cautious of comparison. Nothing stalls this process more than comparing yourself to another woman and how she chooses to show up in the world. Comparison kills creativity. It cripples authentic expression because comparison is rooted in fear; the fear that there isn't enough to go around, and the fear that you are not enough exactly as you are.

Read this slowly; There is room for you.

Whatever it is you want to do, whoever it is you want to be, no one else can do it with your voice, your love, your perspective, your experience, or your insight. What a shame it would be if the world never heard you, saw you, or felt you. Your unique expression is your limitless power. Don't you dare trade that in for a copy-paste version of someone else. Don't you dare give away who you might have been.

"Insist on yourself; never imitate. Your own gift you can offer with the cumulative force of a whole life's cultivation, but of the adopted talent of another, you have only an extemporaneous, half possession."

— Ralph Waldo Emerson

Though our individual paths will all be different, there are certain things that will act as catalysts for every one of us as we flesh out, rewrite the old stories, and give life to our newly re-membered soul bones.

Connect with your body. Return to your senses.

"The body always leads us home . . . if we can simply learn to trust sensation and stay with it long enough for it to reveal appropriate action, movement, insight, or feeling."

– Pat Ogden

Connect with the Earth. Return to the real and natural world.

"Your deepest roots are in nature. No matter who you are, where you live, or what kind of life you lead, you remain irrevocably linked with the rest of creation."

– Charles Cook

Practice presence. Return to the moment.

"Nothing has happened in the past; it happened in the Now. Nothing will ever happen in the future; it will happen in the Now."

– Eckhart Tolle

Express yourself. Return to the Wild.

"If we're really committed to growth, we never stop discovering new dimensions of self and self-expression."

– Oprah Winfrey

Take a moment to write down a few ideas about how you can start establishing a deeper connection with your body and the Earth. Record how you would like to express yourself more authentically moving forward. Take note of any inspiration you have about how you can learn to be more present in your life.

I feel most present when I..

We have discussed in great length the importance of our connection to our bodies, our cycles, our senses, and our sexuality. In the following chapters, we will continue to explore the role that our connection to the Earth, our connection to the present moment, and our connection to ourselves play in returning to the Wild. Aside from these key things, it will be up to you to identify and determine how to most authentically show up and express yourself in this lifetime. You will be the leader on your own path and the writer of your own story. No one else can do that for you, no matter how much experience or expertise they claim to have. What a drag it would be to spend your life reading from someone else's script when you have all the power to write something new. Writing your own story is more than living, it is conscious living. So write it. Sing flesh back onto your bones.

"To sing means to use the soul-voice. It means to say on the breath the truth of one's power and one's need, to breathe soul over the thing that is ailing or in need of restoration... That is singing over the bones."

— Clarissa Pinkola Estes

Returning to the Wild requires that we trust ourselves and our inner knowing. It reminds us that we are the creators of both our internal and external worlds, and that really, they are one and the same. Returning to our Wild selves fosters authenticity and intimacy. By expressing ourselves authentically and living in our most natural, unconditioned state, we are able to profoundly connect to our true nature and our bond to all life. The Wild is where you will access your personal truth, and where you will remember how to be a vehicle for the expression of that truth. Wild Women are the ones who move, change, and direct the world.

"The authentic self is soul made visible."

- Sarah Ban Breathnach

THROUGH

An open promise to myself:
I promise to have you, and hold you, and feel you.
to know you, to grow you, to See you.
to hear you, to heal you, to keep you.
I promise to Be you.

— Indigo

THE CYCLE OF WILD

OF WILD

Both our inner and outer experience is deeply affected by natural cycles of growth and change. We have all felt inner springs, summers, falls, and winters that act as markers on our path of personal evolution, the same way we have felt the shifts in weather as the seasons change. We are part of the endless cycle; Life-Death-Life. This is the infinite nature of creation and expansion, and it is woven within you. By nature you know that you will be reformed and reborn again, and again.

"There is something infinitely healing in the repeated refrains of nature-the assurance that dawn comes after night, and spring after winter."

- Rachel Carson

The evolutionary change we go through as we shed cultural conditioning is a type of "death" that results in absolute rejuvenation. This death allows us to silence and omit the things that do not allow us to be who we are or live the way we desire. To create a new life and embody new form, the old patterns must dissolve and the old form must fall away.

—⁓⊙∿⊂⁓—

"Wild Women: "They know instinctively when things
must die and when things must live; they know how to
walk away, they know how to stay."

— Clarissa Pinkola Estés

When we return to our Wild nature, we are agreeing to actively take part in this cycle over and over again. It is a constant question of what must die and what must live.

What has to die inside of me in order for X to live?

What has to live in order for Y to die?

What has to die so I can experience X?

What has to live so I can have Y?

This shedding and reforming is an ongoing, continuous cycle. In the *Living Temple of Life*, Franklin Gillette beautifully states, "Birth and Death are words we chose to describe the doorways in and out of a cycle. This cycle is connected to a larger cycle which awaits our return." Our existence cannot be divided into two stark events; birth and death. We, like the Earth and all life around us, move through the never-ending, spiraling cycle of Life-Death-Life. It is how our consciousness evolves. It is how we expand and progress. It is the cycle of Wild; the cycle that returns us Home.

"The path isn't a straight line; it's a spiral. You continually come back to things you thought you understood and see deeper truths."

— Barry H. Gillespie

Shedding skin, exhuming bones, and fleshing out are metaphors for phases within this cycle that help spiral you deeper into your personal truths. No path is exactly alike, but as we return to our Wild selves there is one thing we will find that we all have in common,

Everything we were searching for was inside all along.

CALMNESS WIHIN CHAOS

Death is not an end or my demise
But sheds the skin of my disguise
Expands my heart, opens my Eye
And then I rise, I rise, I rise.

—Indigo

Wendeya's Story

If I had the stage, what would I say? What words would I leave as my legacy, or masterpiece of this moment in time? It seems at this moment inconceivable to know what life will manifest as, as only at its completion could I really give the outpouring of my heart, that is considering there is a completion, or perhaps it is the ever unfolding evolution of beginning and endings. Yet in this, it seems like the outpouring of the heart is timeless. Every moment births opportunity for the grand masterpiece that you are to express where it has been and what it holds dearest at any moment. Perhaps that is unchangeable throughout one's existence.

What pours from the most tender parts of my soul is this, I sit here, tears streaming down my cheek as I write, tears from the feeling that overcomes me as I ponder the question, "What is dearest to my heart?" I sit pen to paper watching what my hand will write, I have no idea what is about to pour out of this pen. I watch in wonder as my body translates the immense feelings in my heart, which seem too big to put into words.

Oh the great joy of being Alive, oh the great agony of being alive. To be in wonder as you witness your life unfolding. The canvas and paintbrush are yours, you can create and paint each moment with your brush. Artistically expressing the human experience of each moment.

Often we get in patterns of painting the same stories over and over again. A result of stagnation of the sleeping one who has forgotten the nature of death, and that in this dimension being alive means you are aware of your death. We need this awareness. It serves as a stunning perspective to excite us out of our creation ruts. Showing us a new way to play and interact with the world around us. Gifting us new meaning to paint the canvas with.

The great creator has all perspectives at its fingertips, the ability to comprehend more perspectives enhances the moment of creation as we fill it with artful meaning. It is a great honor to be witness to another's perspective.

In our messiness of being human we express the agony of separation, we express our deepest sobs of ecstasy for existing. We express and make art out of the deepest places in us that can only be expressed with deep art, a language beyond words. Oh bring me to the remembrance of this space, artful communion – from the deepest hollows of my being I pray. This space, where we feel each other and ourselves deeply, where we pluck the most tender heart strings within. You can live like every moment as a masterpiece, you have the power to live in the masterpiece that truly surrounds you, if you will the paint.

Broadening your perspectives deepens the detail of your creation. If you could walk the whole earth and gain a bit of wisdom from every culture, every land, every being, you would have the experience of the God of this world, holding all perspectives and creating from that place. Tune in to that god consciousness, the soul of this world, the great artist. You are a part of that which holds all perspectives.

As a Wild Woman or spark of the Divine Feminine, my expression is always changing, and rebirthing. The artist within creates new versions of herself, the next step in evolution. I have rebirthed new versions of myself many times, and my life shows that. Each new version of myself came with the assistance of those around me as I collected their perspectives. When I was playing the role of Mormon mother and wife, I was surrounded by other Mormon wives and mothers. The person I was being, magnetically attracted a similar vibration to reflect back to me similar perspectives of what I was being, or what my heart's creation was at that moment.

In this lifetime, I have experienced, being a Tantric shaman, Kundalini teacher, energy worker, florist, PTA mom, Waldorf school mom, devout Mormon, Wild Woman, author, ukulele teacher, athlete, medicine woman, and many more roles with unique perspectives.

Each evolution brought me closer to my core. I call it evoluti-OM, where with each evolution births a new version of the self, one closer to home. The evoluti-OM of my ego art brings me closer to the heart with every death and rebirth. With each of these life creations, I was surrounding myself with similar perspectives, it reminds me of the theory you are made up of your 5 closest perspectives. Who do you want to become? And is it reflected back to you? Each time I would die and rebirth, I would attract in the exact people I wished to gain perspective from for the next rebirth.

Once you see the cycle of death and rebirth, you can practice the art of letting go by putting more of yourself on the altar, the more of yourself that you let die, the grander the rebirth. At this point in the game of evoluti-OM the biggest leaps forward come to those who are willing to die, and what identity they are willing to let go of. As women ,we naturally do this with moon cycles, and seasons.

Every creation of the self was loved to the depths, was a full life with deep soul connection as I saw the reflections around me as God and explored their perspective. The grieving and letting go is a huge part of this, and I have come to welcome those feelings as part of the changing seasons in my life. As we walk the spiral feminine path and gain greater perspective with each cycle, we expand our awareness and ability to create the meaning behind the masterpiece of your life. One who is truly free is one who can create whatever they will. This comes with the release of judgment, shedding the skin of who you think you ought to be so you can truly embody whoever the inner artist creates. The key is embracing the ephemeral nature of your creation, knowing that each expression is ever changing, brings more presence and enjoyment to each moment. You have this one life, and it's one blooming open. What will you make of your life? What will your life make of you?

My story of freeing the artist within;

It was New Years Eve 2019 in Joshua Tree, California. My friends and I had gone on a retreat together. I laid down, face in the orange soil. I was begging, pleading for a way out. I laid there thinking of ways to end my life, for the task at hand seemed unbearable. Any direction I traveled it looked like I'd break. At this moment, I would have rather died than moved forward. It felt like there was no other way. I felt so trapped and in heavy despair. I didn't want my world to die, I had four children, and a husband who were my world. I loved that creation with my whole being, heart and soul. I had put everything that I was into that life. Yet the winds of change were here, and I howled like a wolf at the moon, a deep sadness with screeching grief cries.

I had grown up and lived very taken care of by the masculine in my life. I barely had to work. I didn't know what it meant to fully take take of yourself in this world. The seeming objective of these winds of change were to bring me to complete sovereignty. This meant taking care of myself for the first time in my life. I knew I had to leave my family's home and be on my own. The thought was almost debilitating to me, yet I always had everything I needed, and was provided for every step of the way. I didn't know what any of this meant for my relationship, and that scared me the absolute most.

Moving forward was excruciating at first as all of my stories died and crumbled all around me. I didn't know what I was doing or where I was going. I only knew I was following something, something unexplainable, unpredictable, and seemingly destructive. I clung so tightly to the trust in the unknown, the magnetic pulse, it was all I could do.

After I got home from the retreat I vowed to myself that if I was going to "go back" or stay alive, I was going to do everything I could to create aliveness in my life. When I got home my world quickly cracked, I moved out of my family home, and for the first time in my life, had my own place. I had never had my own place before in my life. I had lived with my family growing up, straight to roommates in college, and then to being married. I had never had any alone time. It was the most sacred time of my entire life. My apartment became a cocoon for my transformation, a tomb for the dead me, my space became a reflection of the garden room in my heart, a true retreat from the world, a touch base to my core. A landing pad for zero point.

Making the moves I did caused a lot of tidal waves. Many friends and family stopped talking to me. I was terrified, grieving, and full of this feeling of excitement for the possibilities now open to the mystery. If I would tell you of the agony I felt during that time, it would take songs, and sculptures and poems to convey. If I could tell you of the ecstasy of the blooming open it would smell of roses, scream of rapture, and moan in the unknown. I experienced the

234

234

anguish of my separation to my core. I didn't know what was unfolding. I had to take it one day at a time, and remember to take it moment by moment. There were many wails to the heavens, "Why, what??!!"

I could see how I had brought myself here. I was the one who threw the wild woman retreats, I was the one calling the women to venture into the wild with me. I had channeled the initiations, I followed this inner magnetism through a beautiful intense, wild, sexy, grief filled, initiation process. Yet I couldn't see the end. I didn't know one of the final initiations until I got there....Death. A cracking open, a putting everything you are and have on the altar, giving it all up, not knowing what will be rebirthed. Yet, in it all I grew a deep trust in the process of dying, Trust in what is true will live on, and what is untrue will die. I was scared of finding out what wasn't real, so afraid to put the most precious things to me on the altar.

I was brought to deep states of surrender and letting go. As my old life died, a new one was being rebirthed, it was stunningly drop dead beautiful and everything from my wildest dreams. It was an incredible expansion. It felt like I was being pulled and expanded in every direction, bringing it all home. It expanded my in the most poignant ways as I managed to merge two worlds. Slowly and sweetly merging.

During this transformation that took place, I faced myself in new unknown ways. After a year of gestation in my cocoon, I birthed a new life, I currently live half of the time with my family with my babies daddy, sister, and kids, in a house in a cul de sac in the foothills of the Wasatch Mountains. We call it the East Mountain Ashram. It is peaceful and grounded. The other half of the time I live in an apartment in downtown Salt Lake City with my best friend and we call it The Temple of The Arts. It is a space for artistic exploration. My initiations seem to have led me to be a creator, an artist, and a true lover.

In all the birthing and dying, it brought a remembrance of the sweetness of living, and the shortness of life. It cultivated a deep, deep love for the ones around me. This, is the ephemeral nature of the human experience.

Wendeya Lalla Rose

Eccentric Artist
@WOMANBELOVE

My body, this temple, of skin, blood, and bone

With nature's intelligence, divinely I've grown

To create and manifest through feminine form

Leading with love, I am reclaiming Her throne

– Indigo

EARTH: THE ORIGINAL WILD WOMAN

Forming a deeper connection with the Earth is the simplest way to reconnect with the most innate and Wild parts of yourself, your sexuality, and your soul. The Earth, our physical home, also has the natural ability to guide us home spiritually. She is the obvious gateway to feeling and seeing the connection that exists between all things.

Connecting to the Earth lays the foundation for learning and remembering your true essence and Wild nature. There is a sacred relationship between women and the Earth. Earth is the original Wild, feminine, life-force. When you connect to the Earth you are connecting to divine feminine power both physically and energetically. There is a direct correlation between forming a connection with the Earth and reconnecting to your female body and your divine sexuality. Our physical bodies are chemically and biologically made of Earth. In a very real sense, she is our mother. We are not born into this world haphazardly, we are born out of the Earth. We are made of the Earth and belong to Her. Our very existence depends on the Earth and Her elements.

We will only be at peace with others and ourselves once we make peace with the Earth and our place in it. We are here to live with the Earth, not on top of her. We are not here to dominate or rule. We are here to attend to, care for, nurture, and protect. The subtle reminders of our truest essence and nature are inside the water that flows, the grass that grows, and the creatures left to roam and wander free and Wild. What if you interacted with the Earth and all of life on Earth as if it were a part of you? Because it is.

LE FEMME

We are Gaia. This is not a metaphor.

—Indigo

Being with the Earth allows us to redefine our relationship with ourselves, our natural sexuality, and our innate spirituality. The Earth shows us that you cannot cut spirit from nature, same as you cannot cut soul from body, or sexuality from divinity. Our attempt to separate these things causes immense suffering. All of our pain stems from this disconnection. Heal your connection to the Earth, and you automatically heal yourself. Earth is the first and only real teacher of soulful, connected living.

Your connection to Earth mirrors your connection to yourself and your sexuality. The Earth is as sexual and sensual as we are. We have made sexuality dirty the same way we have made it "dirty" to walk barefoot through the mountains. We are afraid of what might touch us if we do not cover-up. Our unwillingness to connect and be with the Earth has destroyed our ability to connect intimately. It has made it impossible for us to be intimate with ourselves, and as a further result and consequence, impossible to form intimate connections with the people we love most. Though sexuality includes intimacy, intimacy is something that requires far more from us than being sexual. It requires raw vulnerability. It requires naked truth. It requires the most innocent part of your true nature to be seen, touched, felt and experienced. Intimacy is being naked body, mind, and soul and it starts with your willingness to put your feet back in the dirt where they belong.

By healing our separation from nature and our sexuality, we welcome the sacred back into our lives, and return to our Wild souls. In *Sex and the Intelligence of the Heart* Julie McIntyre, reminds us that, "working directly with the intelligence of plants and with all the intelligence and graceful beauty of our bodies, we begin to heal and reclaim the sacredness of Earth, our earthly sexuality, and the bond between them that has been severed…" This bond is severed by a culture conditioned not to feel.

My personal reconnection to myself and the Earth began with exploring Utah deserts, mountains, lakes, hot springs, trails, farms, and was eventually catalyzed by an introduction to psilocybin. I knew enough about mushrooms to understand the possibilities, but not enough to create any expectations for the experience, which was perfect. My little brother took me up the canyon where we had camped and played as kids, gave me five grams and said, "see you on the other side."

He watched over me as I lay down in the sun on a rock by the river, not realizing I was about to have the most profound experience of my life, up until that point. My breath deepened and I melted into my body. The first thing I saw was the face of a court jester, the fool. He was laughing hysterically. "Life's a joke, you're a joke, it's all a joke" he cackled. This bothered me. Surely it wasn't true. I was not a joke, and life was very serious. Or was it?

My eyes were closed, but for the first time, I could see clearly. I began to laugh with the jester, so hard that it brought tears to my eyes. This little plant, in a matter of moments, revealed to me on an inexplicably deep level, how tightly wound I was in a reality that was not mine. The jester came to show me that the personality, rules, and beliefs I had identified with my entire life, were not my truth. This frightened me at first, but the moment I realized (*real-ize: to see with real eyes) that I did not have to live this way, I couldn't help but laugh. Living a life that I hadn't consciously chosen or created was a joke, and I could finally see it as such. I was able to laugh as I shed the layers of limiting and harmful beliefs that had obstructed my ability to be my true self and create my own life.

What followed was a timeless, blissful, and mystical experience. I reconnected with my body, the Earth, my sexuality and my true divine nature simultaneously as the separation between them fell away. For several hours, the intelligence of this little plant worked with the intelligence of my body to open my heart and my mind. I was forever changed. Since then, various plant medicines have served as my most beloved guides, teachers, and friends as I have reclaimed the most sacred parts of myself and returned to my Wild, natural state.

"Forget gurus. Follow plants."

—Terrence McKenna

Our spiritual experiences are here to remind us of who we are so that we can integrate and weave them into our human experience. We are the bridge between Heaven and Earth. With each mystical, numinous, and spiritual experience, we uncover a bone of the Wild self; a piece of what has been forgotten.

"We can choose to move toward the unpredictable, unknowable, and untamable wild. The sacred lives in the wild. The sacred constitutes the wild. The problem began when someone said that words and meanings must explain, domesticate, and cover up wild experience. Within this hegemony of words, we demystified whatever was mysterious and walked away from the wild in order to become semantically tamed. We sacrificed our link-to-the-universe-heart for a delusional body-less-head-trip that has imprisoned us far too long."

—Bradford Keeney

We must learn to recognize our bodies and Earth as holy places. Cultivating relationships with plants and other living things will help us remember, "The body is the temple of the gods and the vehicle through which the soul has life." (McIntyre, *Sex and the Intelligence of the Heart*).

Connecting personally with the Earth reveals and reminds us how to create deep and lasting intimacy within ourselves and our relationships by reclaiming our Wild, spontaneous, and natural sexuality. She encourages us to be vulnerable and open with ourselves, our lovers, and the world around us, thus becoming truly intimate. The wildest place is not outside, but inside of you. Returning to Earth, spending time in her beautiful, untamed places will remind you of that. She is the safest, most honest guide on your path home to your Wild self.

To live soulfully is to live wildly and naturally. Our Wild nature is as ignored, mismanaged, and exploited as the wildlife and wildlands of this Earth. Clarissa Pinkola Estes, Ph.D. writes, "It's not by accident that the pristine wilderness of our planet disappears as the understanding of our own inner wild nature fades. It is not so difficult to comprehend why old forests and old women are viewed as not very important resources. It is not such a mystery." Julie McIntyre in *Sex and the Intelligence of the Heart* again adds to this issue, "The more we take ourselves out of the ecosystem, distance ourselves from nature, and from our own nature, the more unstable we and our culture becomes."

Rather than focus solely on the Earth and our external environment, our attention needs to be directed to our own inner environment first. By healing, connecting, and becoming whole ourselves, we will automatically begin to behave in ways that mend the external environment we have destroyed. It was destroyed first in us.

It only makes sense that as long as we live in ignorance and fear of our own Wild nature, we stand by helpless as the sacred wildlands of this Earth burn, flood, and quake with the pain of our unwillingness to honor and tend to its natural state. Dishonoring the Earth's natural state is an act of dishonoring our own natural and Wild state.

How we treat our environment and the Earth is a perfect mirror of our attitudes towards sex and sexuality, particularly in regard to women, as the Earth herself is a physical embodiment and representation of the feminine. As the Earth was domesticated, so were women. With the growing demand for a "civilized culture" limitations were set upon women the same way boundaries and city limits were drawn to keep things "in check."

"Because the wild is dangerous to so many people's way of thinking, we are taught it must be repressed, suppressed, manicured, trimmed, tamed, cut, sprayed, fenced out, and controlled... Not only did Earth need domestication in their view, but also women, wild and earthy, needed limitations set on their provocative sexual power, their sexual nature... The thing about fences is: when you fence something out, something else is being fenced in."

– Julie McIntyre

It is not a human right to dominate, control, suppress, and extort anything we please. Unfortunately, it is our choice, and it is the one we have made. While on Earth we have been granted the responsibility to tend to, not dominate; to care for, not control. Acting as a superior species will only ensure we become an endangered species. In his work *Of Mystics and Mistakes*, Jaggi Vasudev discusses how, "when conquest became the mode, people burnt the feminine out of the planet. We made it like this that the masculine is the only way to be successful, and we have compelled even women to be very masculine today in their attitude, approach and emotion. We have made everybody believe that conquest is the only way to succeed. But to conquer is not the way; to embrace is the way. Trying to conquer the planet has led to all the disasters. If the feminine was the more dominant factor, or at least if the two were evenly balanced, I don't think you would have any ecological disasters, because the feminine and earth worship always went together. Those cultures which looked upon the earth as the mother, they never caused too much damage to the environment around them."

Clarissa Pinkola Estes gently reminds us, "we see in nature what we have been prepared to see and we feel what we have been prepared to feel. We have been taught to look at fungi, bugs, plants, and animals as lesser life- forms. As a result, we feel and experience our earthly neighbors and our most natural surroundings as dirty, pesky, and savage." We have failed to recognize that Earth is alive, sentient, and aware. As a result, we never learn to see the spirit in the life all around us, and we miss the true essence and deep magic of the Earth, who cares and provides for us without question. It is not just you and I who deserve a Wild, natural life and it is time we act accordingly. Look deep enough and Earth will remind you that when standing face-to-face with any form of life, you will only ever see yourself.

Mending our connection to the feminine by rerooting into a harmonious relationship with the Earth, will be the most revolutionary thing we do in this lifetime. How you see, treat, and choose to be with the Earth is how you will see, treat, and be with yourself and all humankind. What you do to Her, you do to all. My hope is that as we deepen our connection with the Earth, and thereby our true and natural selves, we will shift our attitudes from ownership, "I am in charge of the Earth protecting myself" to partnership, "I am a part of Earth protecting all of life."

The Earth teaches us what it means to be alive. She shows us how sexual, sensuous, Wild, untamed, connected, and free life is meant to be. Earth shows us how and where our Wild souls can be reclaimed. So why do we not know this?

Because we are not slow enough.

We rush around all day long to work, to eat, to travel, and to achieve things outside of ourselves. We are no longer in harmony with the pace and flow of nature. We have forgotten our maker. We have forgotten our home.

Notice your own longing to feel a deep, internal, and natural connection to our living, breathing Mother Earth.

It is not only our responsibility, but our unfulfilled desire to establish and nurture daily relationships with animals, plants, trees, stones, and the elements. As human beings, like every other living species, we are simply another expression of Gaia.

No matter how many walls we build, there is no real separation between us and the Earth. Where would you be without her forests that give you breath, her heat that warms your flesh, her waters that quench your thirst, or her ground that holds and supports you? Reclaiming the body of the Earth and our own bodies as sacred, alive, aware, intelligent, sexual, sensual, and caring, is the most important work we will ever do. Learn to work with the intelligence of plants and with your own natural body, and you will begin to regain your inherent connection with the Earth as you heal the bond that is severed.

This can only happen once you understand that healing is not a thinking thing but a feeling thing. Feeling is the instrument of knowing. To know the Earth and thereby yourself, you must be slow enough to feel. You must walk a sensual path barefoot, naked, and Wild.

SEEKING STRENGTH

Mountains are my Bones
Rivers are my Veins
The Forests are my Thoughts
As Stars my Eyes remain
The Ocean is my Heart
The Wind my subtle Flow
With Earth I'll gently Write
The Music of my Soul

—Indigo

EMBRACING YOUR WILD PATH

Embracing your Wild path means choosing to take the road less traveled. It means you will rarely find paved roads or posted signs directing you which way to turn. It will require you to bring your focus and attention to your internal experience. Instead of relying on others, you will need to determine yourself which steps to take.

*"The human spirit has a primal allegiance
to wildness, to really live."*

– Julie McIntyre

Ombiya's Story

I have always been Wild.

I have never been conventional, and am still lovingly described as, "crazy child" by my mama today.

Even as a child, I was in tune with my sexuality. Even as a child, I was totally mesmerized by sexy music videos on MTV, sex scenes in movies, and touching my own vagina with my girlfriends all through grade school (shoutout to the older girls in grades ahead for the sex ed.) I loved the power and the feeling that would arise from my vagina, filling my whole body with sensation, excitement, and mystery.

I would draw pictures of naked people and hide them in secret places around my room, I'd listen to boy bands and daydream being kissed by them, I'd search nude Spice Girl photos online and sneak into the basement of my friend's house to look at playboy and playgirl magazines. I was more than just curious. I was enthralled. I loved sensuality, especially when it came to the female body.

It was challenging as a young girl because I was taught that all of my feelings, pleasure, sensations, and excitement were "not okay." Because of the cultural shame that has been created around sexuality, I always felt like I needed to hide my desire and love for it.

When something is forbidden, it becomes more exciting and more tempting. I remember being scared to tell my mom about my crushes because I was sure she'd know I wanted to get them naked. And I did. But it was so unacceptable, especially for my age.

I craved physical closeness. I wanted to be kissed, touched, caressed, and pleasured. Unfortunately, my examples of romantic relationships were the love stories depicted in movies and on T.V. My first female role models were the Disney Princesses. This is how I first learned what it meant to be a woman and how to get romantic affection and attention; find the man, fall in love, please the man, serve the man, in order to get to pleasure & feel love.

At only fifteen, I started having sex, but it was never about my own pleasure and always about theirs. How else would I get them to like me? By 16, I had put myself in multiple dangerous situations surrounding sex and drug use. After being hospitalized and suspended from school I was sent away to youth wilderness programs and therapeutic boarding schools. My parents were doing whatever they could to tame me. I understand now that it was simply because they did not have the tools to teach me how to connect to myself, my body, and my sexuality in a healthy way.

As a young adult, I still never wanted to fit into anyone else's mold. No matter what anyone thought of me or told me, I wanted to experience everything for myself and to the absolute fullest. Sometimes, this resulted in me making reckless and harmful decisions.

There was not a single bit of fear that existed in my being, however, I was stuck in the reality that as a woman I would always need to "work" to hold a man's attention. I didn't have the capacity to see myself as a whole and complete human being without objectifying my female body.

Because my youth was void of the support and education I needed to learn to navigate my wild nature, my wild expression became destructive. I chose relationships and situations that allowed me to go wild for a while, but that never cultivated a loving relationship with my sexuality. There is a difference between going wild and being wild. Eventually, I learned a new way to channel this inner Wild Woman, but first I had to completely strip down and get rid of everything I had ever identified with about what it meant to be a sensual, sexual woman.

I sold everything I owned, bought a van to live and travel in, allowed my hair to take its natural curl after straightening it for 10+ years, stopped shaving my body, and stopped wearing makeup. I chose to be celibate for a time and practiced Kundalini Yoga, which helped me reconnect with both my spirituality and my feminine sexuality.

I started practices that enabled me to open up time and space for deep self-reflection. For the first time, I cultivated a strong sense of self and a deep connection to my body.

I learned to channel the same energy and power I looked for in my sexual encounters, into my own passions.

I began to harness and own my sexual power, using it to strengthen my connection to my womb and my intuition. I healed my relationship with my inner Wild Woman. She has since guided me on beautiful journeys around the world, through jungles, oceans, deserts, and mountains. She has connected me to key people who have taught me exactly what I needed to learn and who have surrounded me with so much love and support. She feels safe, seen, able to come out and explore without shame or judgments. I allow new space for her. I respect her. I honor her. I follow her. I love her.

In the early years of my life, my "wild" ways were described as "too much" or "out of control" which I can now recognize is the true beauty of the wild. It has the freedom to move and be whatever it wants to be. It was messy at first because I wasn't ever taught how to connect to this part of myself. I have since learned to grow with it, to channel it, and to let it move through me. Now, I am manifesting my dreams, following my desires, and fulfilling my deepest pleasures. I am living a life where I know I'm going to reach my highest potential, and I can't wait to see all the wild things I do in the future to help change our world & raise the vibration of this planet.

Loving my raw, nasty, seductive, sensual, lustful, Wild power, has brought every single experience I have ever desired into my life and has connected me to the deepest part of myself.

I want all women to know, our wild nature needs to be

embraced & healed, so we can bring this beautiful planet back to balance. Sexuality must be embraced, and our love for ourselves must become unconditional. No more shame, no more fear, just the deepest motherly acceptance, amazement, and love. Embrace the Wild Woman.

Casey Donaldson,

DJ Ombiya Ra

NUTRITION COACH
@WOMANBERAW

$\sim\!\!\sim\!\!\sim\!\!\sim$

"A woman is at heart, a wild creature. But the creature itself... that depends on you."

– Ranata Suzuki

Callie's Story

The journey of coming back home to my most natural, Wild self and embracing my own Wild path involved stripping away everything that was no longer in alignment with me. This began with removing my own IUD in the bathtub one day (note: I am not inviting or encouraging you to do the same, it is simply a part of my story). I wanted to be synched up with the natural rhythms of my body and no longer dictated by a foreign object, or any chemicals.

Then the next step was removing my breast implants so that I could honor my original natural body. The more I tapped into my sexuality, my primal power, the more I realized my heart was blocked, quite literally in this case. I missed feeling myself, my real breasts. I felt blocked. My heart and my lungs were being covered by these implants and the only way I could tap into my sacral energy was by unblocking and taking care of my heart space first. I discovered that the only way I could fully surrender to my sacred, sacral power was by feeling loved and safe in my heart center first. The heart is the gateway to experiencing deeper intimacy with myself and with others.

My breast implants were a physical representation of a time that I did not fully love myself or that I needed this other thing to feel "whole" or complete.

I am not here to shame or judge another being for wanting or getting implants. With the tools and consciousness I had nine years ago I made a choice that "felt good" at the time. And when I made the choice to remove them I experienced more questioning and concern than when I decided to have them put in...

In fact, the amount of questioning, warning against, and recommending I put different ones in was truly perplexing to me. The surgeons I spoke with didn't understand my desire and neither did some of my blood family... and that was ok. I was no longer making decisions based on whether or not others would love me, I was making the most loving decision for myself to love and accept myself fully.

I am grateful for the amount of questioning and resistance, especially from my doctor. Even right before surgery as they were wheeling me to the surgery room, he asked me if I was sure I wanted to go through with the procedure. I was in shock and reacted with, "Why are you doing this?!" He said most women in my situation wouldn't have them removed—they were in "perfect" condition, they weren't causing any health problems, they had another year before they needed to be replaced and could easily have new ones put in. That is the thing though, I am not any ordinary woman. And if you are reading this, neither are you.

I am grateful for all the external resistance I received because it only solidified my "why" and made me realize that this was the right move for me, the one that was in alignment with my highest self and would assist me in the work I believe I am meant to do.

My surgery day was a day of total joy and CELEBRATION. I felt so alive and fortunate to be able to return back to my pure, natural self.

It feels so good to be able to feeeeel myself and fall in love again with my new body.

And I will never forget the moment I saw my breasts for the first time after surgery...the surgeon, with a cold, disappointed tone said, "Well, I hope you like them because that's what they are now." I looked down at them and looked right back at him and said with so much love and gratitude in my heart, "I love them. they're perfect."

Remember, sweet ones, to be gentle with yourself and know that what was once a "yes!" can now be a "heavens no" and that they can both be true. Next time your heart makes a request, I invite you to listen, trust, and act upon that sacred call. Continue to make the most loving decisions for yourself, no matter how big or small and no matter what those around you think you "should" do.

Do what makes you feel gooooooood and what allows you to feel like the most authentic, loving version of yourself- if that's augmenting your human avatar, beautiful. If it's consciously choosing to not wear makeup/adorn yourself in a specific way, that's beautiful too.

Either way, may you feel empowered by your decisions, and know that you are the only one who gets to decide how to navigate your, wildly beautiful life.

My triggers and the catalysts that inspired me to physically remove my implants included choosing out of my four-year partnership. Burning the template, letting go of security, letting go of anything that didn't make me feel fully alive. I was playing a more traditional role that deep down was not setting my heart on fire. Even though I loved my partner and could have stayed in that union, gotten married and continue to play out the contract we had agreed upon, it was no longer my truth, in fact, it was standing in the way of my fullest, most authentic expression and my evolution into higher consciousness. It was not the safe or logical move but it was the most alive and aligned one. And as soon as I said "no" to this template I was able to say "YES" to one that felt like truth, that felt like I was finally on my way home back to myself.

I feel most like a "woman" when I am tapping into myself, my body. When I am dancing, making love, self-pleasuring, playing.

Because I removed what was no longer mine (IUD, implants, four-year partnership), I was ready to be witnessed in my pleasure and play so I started to record myself dancing so that others could see me in my divine femininity and I could practice being seen in this raw, vulnerable state. I love looking back at the dance videos before I made these decisions to physically remove these things that were no longer me from my body, to choose myself instead of my partnership. If I look back and watch those videos at the beginning of my journey, it looks as though I am trying to cover or hide myself within my upper body movements, like I am somewhat timid or apprehensive. Now my movement is more expansive, confident, and fluid. There is a natural, wild beauty and rhythm to my movements on and off the dance floor. I have even had others who have been following my social media, comment on how I have evolved into a more authentic expression of myself.

This journey back home through embracing my Wild path, has allowed me to feel more powerful, sexy, sacred, and ALIVE. And what I have found is that when you are in that vibration of your highest joy, your highest excitement it draws in those who will appreciate you and celebrate you for that. I always say you HAVE to be yourself, your most authentic self at all costs so that those who need YOU can find you.

By stripping away these things that were not me, I could fully express who I really was without any past conditioning or unoriginal templates--I could now call in and receive what I was truly desiring simply by allowing myself to be wild, natural and freely expressed. The men of my dreams, the purest and most passionate play, the heart-altering and expanding experiences.

The question I invite you to ask is, is there something you can shed? Is there something that is not yours or is no longer a sacred "yes" that you can let go of? Are there ways that you aren't showing up as your deepest most authentic self? How can you connect back to your body and lead from your unblocked heart?

Remember, I gave myself permission to do this. I said 'yes' to myself when others were telling me how to live my life. I did this for myself but really I did this for us. I hope that you give yourself permission to honor whatever feels like a sacred yes for you. You are worthy of expressing yourself or showing up however YOU want. By stepping into your power, whether that is through your dance, removing things that no longer serve you, saying yes to yourself you open yourself up and therefore, can receive energy (whether that is energy in the form of money, romance, job opportunities, etc.)

Whatever you choose, choose the thing that makes you feel most ALIVE. Because when you are turned on, life responds to you and all areas of your life will be activated as well.

Callie Bishop

Energy Worker, Guide, & Plant Apprentice

@CALLIEMAEBISHOP
CALLIEMAEBISHOP@GMAIL.COM

If we ignore the roots of our Wild nature and avoid our most natural path, our life will be tamed, limited, and cut short. The Wild asks for one thing and one thing only: that you surrender your heart. True surrender is the relinquishing of all control. For every brave thing, every creative thing, and every inspired thing I have ever done- there has been a moment of complete surrender. And that was when the miracles took place. Surrender your heart and embrace your Wild path. It is here that you will lead a life of independence, freedom, and fulfillment.

PODEROSA STUDY

Let me ask you

Do you know what it means to put your heart on the line?

For Love?

For Life?

For Truth?

Do you know what it feels like to take your whole heart,
stretch it out towards the world and say—
"I am willing to break."

For most people the answer is, "No."
They coddle their hearts
Pretending to go all in, but truthfully,
never giving too much, never pushing too hard, never
opening themselves up to heartbreak; to failure.

They become—
lifeless.

Because unless you are willing to strip yourself down and give your bare, unprotected heart... you cannot know what it is to be alive.

Life is lived with your heart on the line.
It is lived in the fall and the rise,
the break and the mend.

A protected heart is a closed heart.
A guarded heart is a blocked heart.
And that is a heart unused.

A heart unused is a heart wasted.
Pumping blood without purpose,
Beating inside a chest with no soul.

Death does not happen when the heart stops beating
It happens when it beats timidly inside the body of a person unwilling to move, unwilling to risk, unwilling to Live.

This world is not a safe place for your heart. Use it, give it, and it will be broken.
It will be beaten.
It will be cracked and wounded.

But keep it to yourself and something much worse happens

It becomes unbreakable
Un- moldable
Un- lovable
Un- changeable

The hearts that Live have been put on the line— and broken.

The hearts that Live— surrender to the possibility of pain.

So here is my heart

Take it

BECAUSE I AM WILLING TO BREAK

Again and again and again until one day—

My heart beats through the cracks with such ferocity

That I know

What it means to Live.

—Indigo

WHERE THE WILD THINGS ARE

Our environment has trained us to avoid our more subtle senses that keep us present and truly alive. Rather than tune into the intelligence of our bodies, our intuition, our natural desires, and our honest needs, we cram and suppress them with food, substances, entertainment, and countless forms of distraction to numb out from what we would otherwise feel and experience.

We have been civilized to death, meaning, we have traded connection for control. We have traded happiness for a false sense of safety. If we knew how beautiful the Wild truly is, we would never leave it. We would never attempt to escape ourselves for the empty promise that something more lies beyond what we have been naturally given to feel, be, and have in this very moment.

When we can no longer feel or sense our Wild, natural selves, or a Wild and natural world, we disconnect from our purpose and our power. We have become so desensitized, and so afraid to feel that we are almost incapable of detecting how far off balance our world has become. We have not been encouraged to sit with our feelings, but taught to avoid them. We have not been guided to deepen our connections with ourselves and the Earth around us, but trained to build walls of separation. We have not been allowed to seek out a natural way of life, and instead, have been conditioned to accept an artificial experience made up of artificial frequencies, artificial foods, artificial landscapes, and artificial communication, as normal and even desirable.

When we cannot wake up to the fact that the environment we were born into simply does not allow for a connected experience, we struggle to learn how to choose and create an environment that does. Artificial experience is hell on earth. It keeps us in a cycle and system that we would never choose to create ourselves, strung along with the false promise that we are receiving and experiencing civil advancement, comfort, and protection.

This artificial experience is robbing us of our lives. It keeps us in a comfy, steady neutral. Never aware enough to feel too much pain, and never aware enough to feel too much joy. We have flat-lined. This emotional death allows us to coast without exposing ourselves to the lows of disappointment, devastation, and failure. In turn, we sacrifice the highs of immense pleasure, delight, and joy.

We are not present. We are not present, because we are afraid to feel. We are afraid to accept what is. We are afraid of the Wild.

.

"Always say "yes" to the present moment. What could be more futile, more insane, than to create inner resistance to what already is? What could be more insane than to oppose life itself, which is now and always now? Surrender to what is. Say "yes" to life — and see how life suddenly starts working for you rather than against you."

– Eckhart Tolle

Raw, sober presence is what leads to real and lasting intimacy in our relationships with ourselves, with others, and ultimately everything around us. Our ability to consciously choose and create our own reality is dependent upon our level of presence. Presence is what brings us to peak life experiences. It unlocks the world of our dreams, granting access to all we desire to feel and see. Once we come to the realization that now is all we have, every waking moment becomes sacred. Presence is what links and binds spiritual experience with physical experience, and is what allows us to see that they are not separate. With this realization, we find lasting personal joy and through that, create a collective Heaven on Earth.

Connect to yourself in this moment by sinking into your senses. Feel your body, and place your attention on your breath. Can you notice and appreciate the beauty of the exact moment you are in? The shape of the room, the comfort of the couch, your bed, the floor, the clothes you're wearing, and how your body feels loved and held by them, the smell of your home and how it welcomes you, the sound of people walking and talking as they pass, even the taste of your own mouth.

"Presence is not some exotic state that we need to search for or manufacture. In the simplest terms, it is the felt sense of wakefulness, openness, and tenderness that arises when we are fully here and now with our experience."

— Tara Brach

If you have wondered about the purpose of life or our existence here on Earth, it is nothing more than to *feel it.* This is the most profound and obvious, yet elusive truth we have yet to embrace. The whole point of being here on this Earth is to know and feel what it means to be alive; what it is to feel our unique expression as a woman. Life is lived in our enjoyment.

Pay attention to the word *enjoyment.* There are clues built into our language.

En-joy-ment = In-joy-ment = In joy in the moment = Joined with the moment.

When I say life is lived in our enjoyment, I do not mean that life is experienced as joy alone. I mean that life is only lived when we are joined with the moment, no matter what it brings. *That* is the key to real and lasting happiness. It is the only way to live authentically.

It is impossible for us to remain joined with the moment if we are plugged into a system that prefers compliance over creativity, and achievement over balance. Taking control of our own experience allows us to uniquely express ourselves in our individual feminine embodiment. It is what brings us back into our bodies, back into feeling, back into sensuality, and back into the Wild. Your senses bring you back to presence. They bring you back to life!

This is where the Wild things are.

Returning to the Wild means returning to your senses. It means committing to sensual living. It means being fully present. The question is, are you willing to join yourself with each moment? Are you willing to feel it all?

THE LIGHT AROUND ME

(n.) enjoyment: joined with the moment.

This is where the Wild things are.

—Indigo

RESTORING THE WILD LANDS

SKETCH 1

———⟨⟩———

"The future is not female. It is sensual. It is sensual women (and men) who will enjoy the good of the land, or the best of the world."

– Lebo Grand

———⟨⟩———

"The rise of the Divine Feminine does not have to be at the expense of the Sacred Masculine. It is about the complete respect of the differences that the Sacred Masculine and Divine Feminine bring to a physical and spiritual union."

– Reena Kumarasingham

(photo on own page, two quotes on own page)

I want to be very clear that this is not an anti-male book or movement. This is a movement of sovereignty, healing, balance, and restoration for both women and men. We have the unique opportunity to influence the world in a way that will allow all of us to live in more peace, equality, and love together than we have ever previously experienced. While my message is primarily for women, men also have an interest in answering the call of the Wild and taking up the cause of the Wild Woman. Any time a system is thrown out of balance, all parts of the system are adversely affected. When one front tire on a car is underinflated, the entire vehicle is thrown out of alignment, and if not addressed will result in major damage and eventually, a crash.

When the natural Wild nature of women is suppressed, when they are controlled, degraded, hurt, and abused, it not only keeps women from attaining all they are capable of, it also cripples men. It is as if the right leg has shot the left leg in the foot in order to get ahead, not realizing the health and strength of both is necessary for either to achieve its purpose. The metaphors abound for this principle of balance of true divine feminine and masculine power or function. Neither can claim supremacy and achieve victory by suppressing the other.

As more and more men come to realize that they only stand to gain by encouraging women to rediscover and embrace their Wild nature, their lives will become richer, more fulfilling, and their own masculine power will be enhanced. When true balance is achieved, both sexes are able to experience uninhibited joy and pleasure, which leads to a great awakening of higher consciousness.

This begs the question, "How can men help?" The greatest support men can provide is an environment of safety, love, acceptance, and encouragement for all women (especially those closest to them) as they shed cultural conditioning, heal from painful past experiences, and express their natural feminine sexuality. This will require men to go through the same process of overcoming the limiting beliefs and conditioned behaviors that have been passed down to them, and that they have accepted regarding feminine nature, energy, sexuality, and power.

Wendy's Story

My name is Wendy Zane. I live a beautiful life and am married to a wonderful man. One I sometimes still feel I don't even deserve. Especially when I look back at certain moments of my past.

9 years and 2 months ago, I was brutally and repeatedly raped by my boss. I was only 20 years old.

It was my third year working in an intensely male-dominated field. My original boss broke his foot in the pre-season and was replaced by John, a 6'4, 250 lb. tank of a guy-

- and not a good one. I'll spare the details, but he raped me. A lot. It went on for about six weeks, multiple times daily.

I called the company hotline line to tell them what was going on, but they told me that because of how high up he was in the company, that there was nothing they could do.

Suicide wasn't an option. That would mean I'd have to care enough about myself to do something about it. Little by little, I slowly began to die from the inside- out.

None of the crew knew what was happening— John made sure of that. He also took my keys, phone, passport, and driver's license to ensure I couldn't leave. If I made a phone call, he required me to put it on speaker. I couldn't send a text without him reading and approving it first. He called family and friends, put it on speaker, and made me tell them how great of a guy he was. Everyone believed me. He said if I ever told anyone, not only would he kill them, I would have a front seat to the show.

My coping mechanisms (or lack thereof) only compounded the problem. Anything I could do to numb the pain and loneliness, I did. Because I felt used, worthless, and ashamed, I surrounded myself with individuals that fueled the problem. I yearned to feel something---to feel alive---to feel any emotion other than just... darkness. I rode bullet bikes to feel something. I would turn guys on for the sole purpose of being able to tell them, "No." It made me feel like for the first time, I had some control over my life. This went on for years.

It has been just over 9 years since John forced himself into my life and robbed me of my innocence. Though I may never be "over it," as I so commonly hear people say, I try to embrace it and acknowledge it for what it has been in my life—this was an experience that gave me more compassion and love for others than I could have ever fathomed possible.

I wish I could say that I am no longer triggered, but that would be a lie. I can't sit in a room with my back towards the door, I have to have a blanket covering me at all times while I sleep, I double and triple check the locks at night. I am still working through a lot of other things that live below the surface. I have bad dreams and I am afraid he will find me again, but I try not to allow these things to stop me from living my life. I still have a hard time accepting love and feeling love. I second guess my intuition and try to hide my wounds from those around me.

All of this and still-- day by day, moment by moment, I work to replace those fears and triggers and reclaim my life from someone who never deserved a piece of it. I don't want to live an empty-half life anymore. I want and deserve a full life.

I eventually mustered up the courage to report him to the company supervisor and after almost two years of interviews and official statements, they found enough evidence to fire him. I chose not to pursue him criminally.

I often think back to that scared little girl, hiding in the corner of the room before and after she endured unfathomable abuse. I wish I could talk to her. I wish I could hold her and tell her that things will be okay. That her whole future is ahead of her! No doubt, she'll date some scumbags and she'll feel abandoned and rejected by those she once thought were her closest friends....but she'll rise out of it, thriving, not just surviving. She'll rekindle old friendships, create new ones, and end up being in an intimate relationship that's so positive and healthy-- the whole world should be jealous. I'd tell her to hold her head up. That no matter what she does to survive, this was not her cross to bear. It was never hers to carry.

Most of all, I'd tell her I am proud of her. That what she went through is what made me who I am on the other side. I'd tell her there is no one else I'd want to share this experience with. And that I still love her, no matter how she may feel about herself.

While it's not easy to share horrific experiences like this with those who have little or nothing in common, we shouldn't limit our stories by only sharing with those who share a similar history. This isn't a club you necessarily want to be a part of, but cutting out those who haven't gone through something like this prevents us from truly healing. Accepting all the different kinds of people, gender or life experience aside, will help us heal. For example, telling my husband Regan was a game-changer and it brought a level of support and respect I never imagined possible. He has been a huge catalyst to my healing both my relationship with myself and with men in general.

Wendy Zane

Lover & World Traveler
WENDYZANE1@GMAIL.COM

Much of the repressive patriarchal culture, centers around the idea that men must possess and control women. For thousands of years, women were literally considered property with no rights, only obligations and duties towards their husbands (owners). While the laws in most countries have changed, many religious and cultural traditions still persist relegating women to second-class status, subject to the permission and control of men. Men must reject the false and limiting belief that women are to be "controlled" or "possessed" and remove it entirely from all our institutions of culture and tradition.

This can and should start with the most obvious representation of masculine power. Together, we can challenge our concept of God as a "man", who reigns alone in distant heavens as a celibate, non-sexual being with no need or desire for the feminine Goddess. Not only is it metaphysically absurd and irrational, it also sets the entire cultural stage for the denial of the feminine and the suppression of women. In ancient cultures, God did not reign alone in the heavens but was accompanied by the equal co-creating divine feminine principle, personified as the Goddess. Among the Sumerians, Babylonians, Egyptians, Greeks, and even the ancient Hebrews, this was the case. The divine feminine principle was always acknowledged and worshiped alongside her male counterpart. While some of that is still retained in the Christian tradition of the Virgin Mary, Mother of God, it is only a token gesture toward true acknowledgment of the equal importance and place of the Divine Feminine.

***An important note: *"Ancient moon priestesses were called virgins. 'Virgin' meant not married, not belonging to a man- a woman who was 'one-in-herself.' The very word derives from a Latin root meaning, strength, force, skill; and was later applied to men: virle.*

Ishtar, Diana, Astarte, and Isis were all called 'virgin', which did not refer to sexual chastity, but sexual independence. And all great cultural heroes of the past, mythic or historic, were said to be born of virgin mothers: Marduk, Giglamesh, Buddah, Osiris, Dionysus, Genghis Khan, Jesus- they were all affirmed as sons of the Great Mother, of the Original One, their worldly power deriving from Her.

When the Hebrews used the word, and in the original Aramic, it meant 'maiden' or 'young woman', with no connotations of sexual chastity. But later, Christian translators could not conceive of the 'Virgin Mary' as a woman of independent sexuality. Needless to say, they distorted the meaning into sexually pure, chaste, never touched."

—Monica Sjoo,

THE GREAT COSMIC MOTHER:
REDISCOVERING THE RELIGION
OF THE EARTH

Hindu culture comes much closer to maintaining the balance, at least in terms of divine personification of the masculine and feminine principles in Lord Shiva and the Goddess, Shakti. We are also seeing a re-emergence of both Pagan and Hermetic concepts of the divine feminine as the universal life-force principle, the Great "Mother Goddess." Restoring the Goddess to Her heavenly throne alongside her divine masculine counterpart sends the right signal culturally, of the need for balance and acceptance of feminine power in all of our lives. Acknowledging the principles of both the divine feminine and divine masculine is not an invitation to set against and compete as men versus women. Rather, it is an urge to remember that one cannot exist without the other and they are each only as strong as their counterpart. Shifting our concept to both God and Goddess as higher powers teaches us how to love, honor, and worship (serve, work for) these powers and energies within ourselves. Masculine and feminine energy and power present the core principles of all reality, even within our individual souls. We are, all of us, both male and female in that context.

This is not a battle for supremacy, but a quest for balance between these two vital forces that constitute our Universe, and together are the All, the Source; God. As we move to restore this balance, our relationship with both ourselves and our higher power within each of us will expand. It will enable us to understand God as greater energy or consciousness, that is neither he or she alone, but a perfect balance and merging of the two. He and She are the two sides of the same I Am. This whole and perfect power is not independent of you or I. We, as men and women, are expressions of this combined energy and must move to restore its balance within ourselves and our world.

It is vital we remember to not suppress the divine masculine while we learn to re-embrace the divine feminine. Men also play a vital role in bringing about this change in our culture by returning to full vitality and encouraging women to be Wild.

―◯◯∇◯◯―

"Men are called to start building their relationship
with their feminine spirit in order to reverse the
damage that has been caused to the masculine and
feminine energy through patriarchy. The only way for
us to do this, as men, is to start moving closer to the
inner feminine part of our male personality."

—Lebo Grand

A necessary part of the planet's evolution right now lies in women learning to harness their sexual (creative) energy and releasing the shame associated with it. Though the focus is on women, really, it is all of our work. Marianne Williamson calls attention to how this shift has already begun, "There is a collective force rising up on the Earth today, an energy of the reborn feminine... This is a time of monumental shift, from the male dominance of human consciousness back to a balanced relationship between masculine and feminine." As women become leaders in this shift by returning to their Wild nature, men will recognize the need for restoration and welcome it. Our peace is in this balance.

SEEKING STRENGTH STUDY

Notice the peace of Wild things.

CREATING
HEAVEN ON
EARTH

When we answer the call of the Wild, we each do our part in creating a new Earth; a physical Heaven. Your key to Heaven may look different than mine but is no less important. There is a misconception that Heaven and all it promises is reserved only for after this life. This is not the case. By following and fulfilling our life's purpose, dreams, and passions we bring Heaven to Earth in every waking moment.

When you are willing to embody and be what your soul calls to, you bring your unique piece of Heaven to the Earth plane. You are the bridge between dimensions. The secrets to the "kingdom of heaven" are not hidden in books no matter how ancient, classes no matter how advanced, retreats no matter how exotic, gurus no matter how famed, or ceremonies no matter how spiritual. They are inside of you.

When Jeshua Ben David said, "I am the way, the truth, and the light" he was not alluding to the idea that he, as an individual, is our ultimate answer. When he said, "I am the One" he was not implying that he had been given something more than you or I. Rather, he lived his life and spoke these words as a reminder that the way, the truth, and the light is followed and felt inside of the *One;* the balanced center, the collective intelligence of the heart. His urge to "come follow me" has less to do with gaining the attention or the obedience of "followers", and far more to do with providing a model for anyone who could realize (real-ize: to see with real eyes) that the kingdom of heaven was indeed inside themselves. I use this as an example because it is the most widely relatable. It is also the most widely misunderstood.

Every spiritual leader gave their lives to help us remember and understand that there is nothing to find outside of ourselves. There is nowhere to go but in, nothing to do but be here now. Heaven is not somewhere we go when we die, rather it is a state we can create in any time, place, or reality by returning to our true divine nature. We create Heaven on Earth by returning to the Wild. It can be accessed and enhanced at any moment, provided we don't object to it.

Unfortunately, our actions and beliefs indicate that we do object to this. We are either stuck in events of the past or racing towards events we hope will be in our future. We are not present long enough to be our true and natural selves. We are either mourning who we once were, or chasing someone we'd like to be. The only way to free ourselves from the suffering we create by living in the past or by chasing the future is to shed the past and surrender to the Wild, present moment. It is only in the here and now that we can create and live the life we desire.

It is as possible to create joy (living in the present), as it is to create pain (living in the past or chasing the future), although no less vulnerable. Creating Heaven on Earth (presence) requires the same amount of effort as creating Hell on Earth (endless suffering created by living in the past and/or future; mind games; artificial living). One is simply done consciously while the other is not. Creating Heaven on Earth requires you to BE HERE NOW. It requires your love, your passion, your play, and your power. It requires the best you have within you because Heaven IS the best you have within you.

Our human experience is sacred and significant. Our human lives are deeply spiritual. The spiritual and the physical are not separate, though we train ourselves to experience them that way. Your day-to-day life is a spiritual practice. Your human experience is a spiritual practice. Meditation, yoga, reading, writing, dancing, painting, and music are all things that help to strengthen a connection to the sacred, spiritual world that exists all around us. When this is done, showering, getting dressed, doing the dishes, your work, and how you move throughout the day can become spiritual acts of self-care as we learn to be more present in each moment. When we are Wild, we can breathe magic into the mundane. Our awareness of and attention to ourselves and our individual experience is what allows everything to become deeply spiritual and significant. You begin to realize that nothing you do is passive or unimportant.

We must return to the Wild. Our nature as women, as human women, is the most sacred and holy thing we have. The Wild connects us back to the spiritual. It allows for the collective co-creation of Heaven on Earth. The reason we must begin identifying and abandoning our cultural conditioning is because it is impossible to be truly present when our minds are full of the guilt, shame, resentment, and fear handed down from the past. So, strip. Get naked with me, truly naked. The most important characteristic of paradise was, "they were naked and not ashamed."

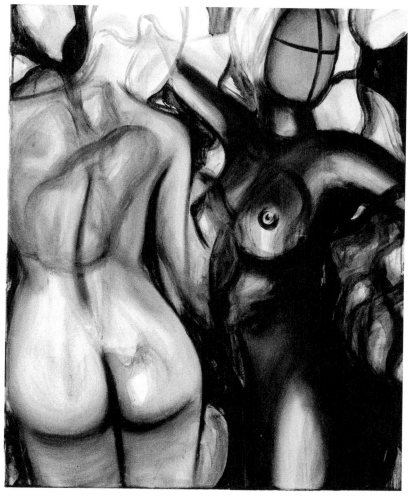

LET'S DANCE

Heaven on Earth is built as you practice and pursue your greatest passions. If your passion is painting, the more present you are, the more the Wild will move through you as your brush strokes the page. If your passion is music, the more present you are, the more the Wild will flow through each note as you play. If your passion is writing, the more present you are, the more the Wild will drip from every word. If your passion is photography, modeling, dancing, coaching, childbearing, traveling, or business building, the Wild will leak into every present step you take along your path.

By living in your joy, in your moment, you will change the world. The more willing you are to embrace and fully embody your innate desires, the more you become a beacon for others to do the same. Woman, the world will feel you. Lead them home.

FLOW

Give the world your heART.
let Love leave its mark.

—Indigo

Were every one of us to find the courage to relentlessly and fearlessly pursue the deepest desires of our hearts, not only would it create a personal Heaven on Earth for each individual woman, it would restore a world so gravely lost to patriarchal control and imbalance. Woman, your work is so much greater than you know. Heaven is created and felt when we fiercely devote ourselves to our own unique path of joy. Imagine if every woman stopped bolstering the dreams of others and poured themselves into their own passions and offerings. We would become the weavers of dreams.

If you want to shift, change, and create your reality, pick up your pen and write, connect to your body and dance, capture the most beautiful moments you see and share them with the world. Express, express, express. Expression is how we shine light onto dark and free joy to heal pain. Your unique expression bridges the gap between heavenly and earthly states of being. It is what creates a reality where they are one and the same.

Wild, authentic expression is divinity embodied. Your unique and authentic channel of expression is what links you to the divine. It is how you bring your piece of Heaven to the Earth and is what allows you to feel as if you are in Heaven while on Earth. The soul seeks Wild, unbridled expression. If we are not connected to our natural, Wild, feminine nature and if we are not free in our sexuality, we cannot be who we came here to be or do what we came here to do, because we are cut off from our Source of divine and infinite power. Your expression is the light of the world and you are the source of that light.

It is your life's work to bring Heaven to Earth by being and expressing all that you are. You are the SOULution.

"A succulent Wild Woman is one of any age who feels free to fully express herself in every dimension of her life."

- SARK

Tkayah's Story

From my first memories, I had a knowing that there was always more than what I was able and taught to perceive. I knew that *I* was more, and that I was here to access and initiate that awareness.

I was raised in a deep line of the LDS religion on my fathers side, which crafted and molded my understanding and ability to feel truth and spirit. Although it came with heavy dogmas and shame laced through my "agency to choose." I have catholic blood as well, although my mother and her mother embodied free spirit, and did not adhere to any dogma - instilling me with passion and open perspective of nature and life instead. I was blessed with such a perfect balance in my family dynamics.

My mother left my father when I was six years and my brother was two. From then on, I was thrust into a *yours, mine, ours, & theirs* type of experience. Being the oldest was a blessing and a challenge, that I graciously accepted and lived to the best of my awareness. So much responsibility to be the 'example' and the one who my parents were learning how to raise first. Of course I would fulfill that role, I see now. But as a young and teenage girl, I had a difficult time forming healthy attachments with love, and healthy relationships with my body and the vessel that I have been *gifted*. I knew deep in my heart this power and royalty that has always been fractaling through my DNA, and yet, I felt such unworthiness and such deep shame due to the conditioned misbeliefs that have been acquired by my experiences, and handed down from those before me. I honor you, thank you.

When I left my home in Meridian, Idaho for college in Utah, I had only just begun stepping outside of this perfectly crafted "mormon girl" role. I had dabbled in all the naughty things and was ready to go live my life! Little did I know that I would be facing some pretty dark and challenging experiences. This looked like traumatising and hurting myself - from my need to be validated by everyone and everything outside of my own self, my heart, my body.

There was a time that I suffered a dark night of the soul: Alone, in my home, curtains drawn. Covered, vulnerable, raw, nothing to distract me from my emotions, and my unraveling. I was lost. Disconnected. I hated myself. I hated my body, and my desire to just be wanted *really*.. I had experienced the true darkness of my shadow-self not knowing of Her inherent divinity.

In those moments, I called upon God, Spirit, Anything, The Creator of All that Is from my heart and soul, which was something I hadn't done in years. And I was met, and answered. I listened. I got myself up right then and there, and took action. I read and studied the ways of other systems, philosophies in countless books and documents; I wrote. I found my Spirit -the nectar of Source- again between the words on the pages of those books, and between the lines of my own writing. Remembering who I have always been.

From those moments, Arose a beautiful path of shadow work, embodiment, play, fierce love, undoing, recreating, liberating, contracting, expanding, and the most profound s e l f healing.

What I would have given during the moments of deep challenge to have someone shake me into remembrance of what has AllWays been Me: *Divinity Embodied in All form/ formlessness Being.*

THIS IS ALL OF US, HELLO.

I returned to the divine purpose of my soul, and I chose a series of Now moments that guided me to the most full-filling mission and actualization of infinite immortal prosperity that I could have dreamed up with my ascended masters and higher self. I chose to devote myself to Source. I chose to devote myself to my body, my truth, my wisdom, and my right to be exactly where I am. I chose to leap into spaces of discomfort so that I could expand, and be opened by life even more - there is AllWays more.

Since I came home to this knowing and knowing no thing, I have felt truly liberated to my fullest potential and loving awareness. I have been able to witness myself heal my body, mind, my DNA, ancestral lineage, genetic frequency bands and fractal patterns beyond time and space.

I have been able to live my dreams, and witness those who come into co-creation with me do the same. A biofeedback loop of manifestors and dreamweavers, who are making the TRUTH come alive through embodied being. Celebrating every moment of living: I AM All that Eye AM. Owning All Parts of ourselves. Making love with life. Listening and Communing. Feeling our bodies - actually. There is wisdom for us in every cell, in every molecule, proton, neutron, and electron there is a knowing of our true purpose, our DIVINE inherent nature. It is time to remember these truths and return to our natural, wild, Essence.

TKayah Bell

Sound Healer, Reiki Master, Fire Dancer
@WOMANBESOURCE

Your connection to the All, the Universe, to Source, to God, to Gaia, Spirit, Sophia, your Higher Power *IS* your connection to your feminine center. You can only connect with Her when you are totally free of worldly imbalances and limitations. The true nature of God is *balanced and limitless*. When you learn to see God, you learn to see Yourself.

The deeper I have looked into the eyes of God, the more clearly I have seen myself reflected back to me. God is not only a Power, it is a state of Being. It is a state of pure Love. When you become whole and balanced in this state, you will know who you are. Love lives in expression and expression moves through our unique embodiments. You, as a divine, spiritual being, a piece of God, chose to express and move Love through you this time, as a Woman.

How will you embody Love?

How will you live in a unique, unbridled, limitless, and Wild way?

How will you express and move in presence, on Earth, as a Woman?

DESENREDANDO

Love is the whole thing, and we are the pieces.

WOMAN
BE WILD

I believe that women have a specific and special role to play on the Earth in reclaiming the Wild and restoring balance in our world. I believe that this work is an indispensable contribution to the healing and transformation of the entire planet. When a woman connects to her most natural state, her Wild essence, and roots herself in her own sensuality, she gains access to higher dimensions and becomes a bridge between realms. It is little wonder that the female body was chosen to usher souls into the world. This is a literal representation of the power and purpose of the feminine essence we embody. It is feminine energy that can and will raise the vibration of the entire planet when balanced and integrated.

The valley spirit never dies;

It is the woman, primal mother.

Her gateway is the root of heaven and earth.

It is like a veil barely seen.

Use it; it will never fail.

—Lao Tsu, Tao Te Ching

Until we return to the real root of our nature, we cannot rise to our limitless potential. A false root, or a false idea of feminine nature, breeds a poor idea of who women are and what they are capable of. It keeps us from ever knowing or being who we really are and results in feelings of helplessness, disconnection, frustration, and discouragement. If you have not experienced a life full of purpose, meaning, passion, and fulfillment, and find yourself searching for something more, it is because you have not sunk back into your Wild roots.

We will never progress by fighting the existing model. What we resist, persists. We need not oppose the existing model, but instead, work to return to our natural state. As we do this, we free ourselves from this broken model and can create something together that renders it obsolete.

You are not meant to follow the society you were born into. You are meant to inspire it, to teach it, to change it, and to create it.

We did not come here to live in a cage of culturally imposed limitations. We came to be Wild. It is the natural way.

Bound by no boundaries, contained by no countries,
tamed by no time, she is the force of nature's course.

— Roman Payne,
The Wanderess

The suppression of the feminine is severe and extensive, but it is not insurmountable. If we each heal our understanding of and relationship with the Earth and our sensual bodies, we will reroot into our true nature and be able to fully embrace our feminine sexuality. Standing fully in our feminine sovereignty and power, we join our presence with the mystical and unseen world that connects us to all things.

Gaining an understanding of the interconnection between the Earth, our feminine sexuality, and our Wild nature, is the key to living a life of joy, purpose, and fulfillment. It is only through our connection to these things that we can live a life of true freedom and independence.

The purpose of this book is to help you begin your own feminine awakening process by shedding the social and cultural conditioning that inhibits your ability to live as you were meant to live. It is also designed to help those of you who have already begun this process, to embrace your feminine sexuality and continue on your path with more clarity and confidence than before so that you can be a beacon and inspiration for this Wild, feminine revolution.

My greatest hope is that the women who read this book become guides and teachers in awakening others to return to their Wild, authentic selves. Often, the women who are most helpful are not the ones who are leaps and bounds ahead, but those who are only a few steps in front of you. Find the women near you who share a similar vision. Support each other, guide each other, love each other. We are all in this together.

Wherever you find yourself on your path, the most important thing is to continue. Move forward, onward, upward. Transcend your limits.

Wild things never stop growing.

IT WAS ALWAYS THERE

Woman, Be Wild.

YOUR
STORY

It has been said that those who tell the stories rule the world. My hope is that somewhere in this book, you felt compelled to take charge of your own life and inspired to consciously write your own story. Now, I would like to encourage you to share that story, even if it doesn't feel complete- because the truth is, it never will. Tell it as you live it and share it with the rest of us. I asked several of the closest women in my life to write their stories of returning to their most Wild, natural selves which required them to share some of their most vulnerable moments, their darkest times, and their deepest pains. Though these stories are ultimately powerful and positive, what I asked them to do was not easy. Writing brings a lot to the surface because when we write we are doing more than just thinking about an idea or situation. When we write and share our stories, we are required to feel deeply stored emotion. We are required to process things we may have ignored, travel to places where we have buried pieces of ourselves, and face the things we have tucked away to avoid fear, shame, guilt, regret, embarrassment, and grief. To tell our stories, we are required to make the unconscious, conscious. Writing is an act of conscious living. We are here to powerfully and consciously write Herstory.

"Become aware of what is in you. Announce it, pronounce it, produce it, and give birth to it."

– Meister Eckhart

Below, I have included an unedited conversation that unfolded between one of my dearest friends and I after I asked her to share her story for this book. We wrote back and forth addressing the feelings that came up for her as she dove inward and began the process of reconnecting to her natural Wild Woman. It is a raw and authentic representation of what goes on inside each of us as we begin to consider our natural state, and question what conditioning exists in our lives that needs to be shed in order for us to be the women we are meant to be. It also perfectly and sweetly demonstrates how different our paths are and how those differences matter and deserve to be honored. What an incredible thing it is to be here on Earth together, as women, expressing the Wild feminine in as many different ways as possible.

Bailie's Story

As I sat here and contemplated my womanhood I closed my eyes and I thought, "dammit why won't you ever help me write anything?" All you ever say is, "write from your heart." I hate that answer because A.) it just sounds better when you write it and B.) I'm lazy. But I know you are right. So I sit here stoned, watching shows about kings and queens, drinking tea, and writing a letter. A gift to you as I read your book.

Normally, I am a total ADHD reader. I carry around four or five different books in one of my bags and am continually interchanging them, reading random parts from each, and it's all over the place. So, I love a book that is strong enough to keep my focus, and yours has.

It has been hard to write because I am realizing that I have a lot of work to get back to my raw and natural state.

Bailie,

Instead of trying so hard to write your "story", I would love for you to focus first on this feeling. What made this come up? What did you read that made you feel this way? Many of the readers are going to feel this way, and I would love for them to have the opportunity to relate to you as you express your thoughts and feelings here as you write in real-time. Let's explore this in more detail. We can let it be an open conversation.

The sad yet beautiful truth is, I am realizing that I still have yet to find myself as a woman. In fact, I am just beginning. I am now realizing that fully embracing and stepping into my feminine power is the greatest love and gift that I can give not only to myself but to my husband, my king.

So I will do the work.

I have all of this information. All of these bits and pieces from experiences and lessons in my life where I have seen things that I know I either like and want to replicate, or don't like and should discard.

Getting back to my raw natural state involves me working through a few things, organizing my experiences and reflecting on what I have learned from them.

My experiences with religion and where I stand there.

When I think of sexuality I think of my past sexual experiences and how those affect my raw natural state.

How to view and process my past sexual relationships with other women.

How to view and process my past wild nights with men.

Was I too loose? Was that important in my journey?

How to express my sexuality now as a married woman.

Here I am reading your book. Loving it. Feeling it. Thinking yes, this is me. I feel this way. I yearn for freedom from all limitations. But then suddenly, I feel as if I am different.

As I read about how you have shed your layers of false

beliefs and limited cultural conditioning, I stopped and thought to myself, "do I have to strip myself of all religious beliefs in order to find myself?"

My feeling is, yes. Joseph Smith (the founder of the religion you associate with) and every other religious leader also felt a resounding, "yes." They did this personally. Often in church classes, we are guided to "be like them." What does this really mean? I wonder...

I feel and have found that if you are willing to do this with faith that you will face and accept YOUR own personal truth whatever it turns out to be, you will find more personal peace than you ever knew possible. Belief is clinging to what we've learned. Faith lets go.

What if you could have the faith that NO MATTER WHAT- you are going to end up exactly where you are meant to be?

Can I find myself in the same religion that was holding you back? And further, can we still maintain a friendship in all of this?

It's not about whether or not religion is right or wrong. The real question is, has it kept you from exploring yourself, your concept and relationship with God, the universe, etc. in any way? This has less to do about the future of our relationship, and more to do with your present relationship with yourself which impacts your entire future.

How can I similarly have different spiritual views from my husband, and still respect how we each feel?

The most loving thing we can do for other people (especially those closest to us) is to allow the space for them to choose differently than we would choose ourselves. If you can both do this for each other, imagine the safe, supportive environment you could create for yourselves and your future family.

My spirituality seems to be at the center of this, is what I am finding out.

Of course, it is. Because you are a spiritual being.

The first time I can recall checking in with my spirituality vs. sexuality was in college. Why do I feel like it is a war or a battle? Can't everyone just get along? I think that is what I really want, for my spirituality and my sexuality to feel aligned.

We have been taught to compartmentalize our lives into categories (ie spiritual versus sexual) when really, they are not separate. They are inextricably woven together. Our very nature is both spiritual and sexual. How could we cut ourselves in two and still feel whole?

So then I am not trying to get them to align, but rather the realization that they are one, and how to make that work. How to let each have a voice?

Aligning what you are currently viewing as two separate things would indeed unify or make one. My next question is, who do you think the two different voices belong to? What if the two "voices" you are hearing is the voice of the "conditioned past" arguing with your true and natural self?

I love reading about experiences that have helped you reconnect with your inner woman, or the Wild as you call it, yet I have a hard time articulating how I feel about mine.

I think it is important for me to say here, that for a long time I felt stifled by the idea that I could not articulate my own feelings and emotions as well as other women could. For example, being such great friends with you for so many years has taught me so much about how to better express myself, but it wasn't always easy. I seem to always be surrounded by women who can speak or write or define how they feel and what they want with so much detail. So in that regard, my sense of self and my desires were dependent upon my ability to write or speak about them. I don't feel like I am there yet. What advice do you have for us women who are working on self-expression?

Find the willingness to be imperfect. Take messy action. Feel the fear and do it anyway. When you feel something tug at your heart, write it down. Ask yourself why it mattered. When you feel your stomach flutter during a conversation because you have something important to add- say it. Add yourself and your light to this world. Make it a spiritual practice. Honor yourself and your feelings by sharing them with the world the same way you would share something sacred with those around you; share it with faith that it will do as much good for them as it will for you. Ultimately, what you write and what you say will be remembered only in fragments. The real significance is what you and others feel as a result of that expression. You have no idea how much impact your voice can have.

I am now realizing that at the center of my inner feminine, or wild nature, is a place where my spirituality and sexuality are one. This is how you have reconnected with your inner feminine presence, and is it okay that I also connect with my feminine presence in different ways, and that doesn't make yours or mine wrong.

You're right. Women, by nature, fit no single mold. I sense that the reason you are feeling this desire for your sexuality and your spirituality to be "one" is because by nature, they are. Somewhere, at some time, you were taught that they weren't, and may have even been taught to pit one against the other in some ways. The truth is, (and I think you already know this deep within you or you would feel so much discomfort) that our sexuality is deeply spiritual because it is the bridge back to our Source. Sexual energy is creative energy. It is what we came from and what we must return to in order to fully express our true selves.

Why am I so shy to share my beliefs and wants when

they contradict with others? I know you have found a lot of joy and freedom from leaving a more restrictive religious environment. I like the same religion you left. Is that bad? No, it's not. You have taught me that. It can be a yes for me, and a no for you. It's beautiful to understand that. That is what I love about our friendship, and why I love your energy and presence, is because you are a true woman. You are a safe place for me to share my inner desires, even if I feel like they are not popular. So as I read or listen to all of these beautiful women's stories, it is a good reminder that as a woman, I must always be in tune with what I want, and know that I have my own barometer.

"I have changed the world because I have changed *my* world." I read this in your book. It is poetic and beautiful and gives me so much clarity. My mind runs wild with this thought.

What an interesting thing it is to realize, that your world is the only world you experience. Changing how you perceive and connect to the world around you and how you relate and connect to yourself, changes your experience which changes your entire life. The way a caterpillar experiences life is very different than the way a butterfly experiences life. It's a whole new world.

As I read this book, I started to think about my natural state. I want to strip everything away, and still be religious. Can I do that?

My advice is to strip everything down especially in areas you feel most resistant to do so. In this instance, religion. Explore beyond what you've been taught and what you think you "know." Drop your own limitations. Focus on your feelings and new spiritual experiences. Release the need to spin in the overthinking of old religious habits.

Where do I start? For example, a big inner conflict for me is smoking marijuana and drinking coffee. Those are the two things that stand between me being able to go into the temple (a religious practice I like to participate in). How should I feel about that? Honestly, right now I am pretty neutral. You know me, I love to smoke a good bowl before bed. Or wake up to a sunrise spliff and yoga-sesh. I think it is okay that I still want to be religious and smoke weed and I don't feel bad about it at all honestly, but I do feel weird when I wonder about how discrete I need to be about it. Should I be loud about it and post pictures unapologetically? Or Should I lie about it? And which would be true to my soul and inner wild? Because initially I am thinking that I want to be a classy woman and I am a pretty private person. I don't necessarily want to lie about smoking weed because I am embarrassed or think people will judge me but I am naturally more cautious. I wouldn't smoke right in front of my grandma if she came over. Is that me not being true to myself? Or is that being true to myself in the respect that I love and respect my elders and I am socially aware of what's going on?

I would start simply. Knowing that you can pick it all back up later if you want, what if you started by really wiping the slate clean? What if you dropped everything completely and approached this as if everything you know is wrong... everything. New day, new Bailie. What is she choosing? And why is she choosing it? Is she choosing things out of obligation, habit, or because she learned they were the "best" for her? Or is she choosing things because they feel good, they are uplifting, and they are things that allow her to enjoy life to the fullest? I can't tell you if you will be happier smoking weed or attending the temple- that's for you to decide. I also can't tell you which is more spiritual. Some of my most spiritual experiences have been with plants. Their medicine is remarkable. My point is, this decision cannot be made purely by you until you let go of what you were taught by other people, organizations, institutions, the media, etc. Feel into it. Really feel into it. Let your body guide you. Our bodies can't lie. They don't know how to lie. And, you're the only one who can feel your body. Start there.

As far as being true to yourself by sharing what you are doing or not doing with the rest of the world, again, this is entirely up to you. This has less to do with self-expression and more to do with inner peace when it comes to certain behaviors. I like to smoke as well, but it is not part of my identity. I do know women who are passionate about sharing their love for this little plant. It seems to become a part of their self-expression because of the peace and presence it has brought to their lives. This isn't something I feel the desire to personally share, but it also isn't something I hide. My behavior and expression with it is in balance for me personally- not based on anyone else's preferences or opinions. Find your balance.

I want to make different choices in the future and laugh about some of the choices I've made in the past. How do I return to my wild, natural state while still loving and accepting my breast implants? How do I love and accept myself, yet still yearn for improvement?

Just like something that is a "yes" for you may be a "no" for me, something that was a "yes" for 22 year-old Bailie may be a "no" for 30-year-old Bailie. This doesn't mean we don't like 22-year-old Bailie. Or that we're mad at 22-year-old Bailie. We love 22-year-old Bailie! She was choosing and acting with the experience and perspective she had. 30-year-old Bailie may have more experience and a new perspective. This doesn't make past choices bad, wrong, or unlovable. They're a part of our ever unfolding path and should be embraced as the powerful stepping stones they are. Those choices are part of what brought you to where you are now. Love them for that, accept yourself in all stages, and move forward with as much love as possible. Something I like to do when I am making even the smallest decision is ask, "If I loved myself, would I _____?"

If I loved myself, how would I feel about my breast implants? Well, I actually secretly love them. I finally came to the conclusion that if I have them and love them, I also want to show them off. I should start showing more cleavage. I just decided that as I was writing. Because that's really what I want to do. It is unraveling right here before our eyes ladies and hopefully gentlemen reading this out there. I love my boobs, they are sexy and full and make me feel like a woman. For years I felt like I had to hide them or that since they weren't 'natural' I couldn't be proud of them and you know what, that just simply isn't the case. They have given me so many moments of feeling sexy and delicious and amazing and I am so grateful for them and I need to let them shine more.

Woman, be wild ;)

As I speak to so many beautiful, powerful women, including you, I realize that a lot of their feminine power comes from "breaking free" from things that are tying them down. How can I relate with someone who has found freedom from their toxic relationship, and simultaneously, enjoy a relationship that really completes me? The truth is, I'm really getting to the root of things as I write about this, and I'm feeling that the things that make me feel most at home, are often the very things that tie people down.

I believe this is because on a deep internal level, you have felt less "tied down" in your life than most. You are a natural Wild Woman. That's probably where some of this confusion comes in. She has always been present with you. That "inner Wild" or deep inner feminine has always been strong and kept you on your own path no matter what was going on in your immediate environment. It is easy for you to feel your natural independence. Even if you were taught certain things, they didn't "stick" to you or become a part of your identity like they do for so many others. It is possible that this is why you don't experience a similar feeling of being suppressed or controlled by certain ideas or situations.

I really love having a relationship with God and being a part of a religious community. However, a lot of my good friends, including you, have felt repressed by certain religious bounds and really have found yourself after releasing the "religious shackles" so to speak. So then I am left feeling like, well, I have tried to do the same, stripping off the conditioning and seeing how I feel, and for me, it's a "yes", and I think that is the biggest thing about womanhood that I need to fully understand better, and that your book is teaching me too, is that I can find my inner woman and still incorporate having a religious practice.

Questioning what we were taught about God in church while we were growing up does not mean we are stripping away our relationship with God. It means we are giving ourselves the power, permission, and opportunity to redefine it, to expand it, and to deepen it.

It's a similar feeling on my journey finding myself while in a committed relationship with Brennan. So many of my friends and family have found freedom independently of a man. They have found themselves once they step away from a relationship or a situation. I feel the opposite. I feel complete, powerful, and protected. I feel free to place my boundaries and speak my desires. To chase my dreams and do what I please. I am his queen and I have loved finding myself, finding my inner woman since getting married.

This is likely because you are experiencing a balance with masculine and feminine energy inside your relationship. This is what we all search for in any relationship. The masculine's role is to ground, protect and hold space for the Wild feminine. If Brennan does this for you, thank God! You're in a relationship where you can safely and fearlessly lean into your Wild feminine nature. What a blessing! This is what I believe many women feel unsafe to do in relationships (or they are unknowingly incapable because of codependent tendencies), which is why it takes being away from a man to be their best selves.

I am still figuring out how to incorporate my spirituality within my relationship. Brennan doesn't like to be "strapped down by the bounds of religion" or however you want to say it. I love being active in a religious community and forming these close bonds with people around me. I love meeting weekly and singing together.

I love what you've said here because these are things we all love and yearn for. Community is important and routine is important, especially in spiritual practices. There is a reason every religion has some sort of ritual. Ritual preps our consciousness to connect with realms "beyond". Whatever helps you feel fulfilled here is wonderful. I think what Brennan and I, and many others mean by "tied down" is that for most religious organizations, they ask you to rely upon the stories and experiences of others. There is one "correct" interpretation and with that, a certain set of behaviors that are expected to be repeated for all time and by all people. This is limiting and begins to feel that way for a lot of men and women. We should all be encouraged to rely upon our own experiences, to interpret things for ourselves, and to pave our own path and cultivate our own relationship with God. I think the reason you have never had a problem with this inside of a religious organization, is that you have always trusted in your own experiences and not allowed the religion to limit them (sex, weed, mushrooms, etc). If there is a balance here you can find and enjoy- amazing!

Sometimes I feel like I can't be myself because something that brings me joy, happens to also be this huge controversial thing for some of the closest people in my life. Their detachment from the thing I love becomes the keystone of their freedom, and I feel the actual opposite.

I even downplay the importance of things like religion or hesitate to speak my mind at times in my marriage because I fear that I will lose Brennan because of it. And if it came down to being an active participant in a religious organization that has brought me so much joy and guidance, or having Brennan as my partner, I would choose Brennan every single time.

Anytime we act or don't act out of fear, we lose our power and our authenticity. Your authenticity and individuality are what Brennan fell in love with. It hurts both of you in equal degree to allow that to dwindle for any reason. Just like you and I, you and Brennan don't have to agree on everything. How boring it would be if you did. You entered into a marriage to love and support one another; to be partners- not to be one person. A lot of the work in a partnership is seeking to understand the other, and then doing things that support their individual desires. Not everything you two do will be exactly alike. Just because you are married, doesn't mean you aren't also still a sovereign soul on your own personal path. The same goes for him. Allowing space for this in relationships is what I think, the greatest secret for sustainable happiness as partners.

I don't like that I was somehow conditioned and trained that my love and marriage for my future husband should be dependent on his activity and faith in the church. That is just nonsense to me. I believe spiritual activity is such an individual thing. Which is what I believe you are trying to teach me. That it is okay for me to say that I love to be religious, and to want to incorporate that into my life. It is okay for me to say that I get a lot of my power and strength from the man in my life and that he is a fuel-source for me. And that it is also okay that people do have the same feeling about removing a presence from their life and that is okay too. This is how you have reconnected with your inner feminine presence, and is it okay that I also connect with my feminine presence by strengthening my relationship with God, and that doesn't make yours wrong, but why am I so nervous to share that with my friends or family.

"But why am I so nervous to share that with my friends or family?" This would be a great thing to journal about.

I want to point out that connecting back to your feminine nature is never void of strengthening your relationship with God, in fact, it is quite the opposite. I believe what may be confusing is that we have a different concept of God and who/ what God is. This is of course, okay. It is perfect. However, I would never separate embracing your feminine power and strengthening your relationship with your higher power. One can actually not be done without the other.

That is what I love about our friendship though, and why I love your energy and presence, is because you are a true woman. You are a safe place to share my inner desires, even if I feel like they are not popular. So as I read or listen to all of these beautiful women's stories, it is a good reminder that as a woman I must always be in tune with what I want, and know that is enough.

Sometimes there is a lingering little voice, something we picked up from someone else that made us feel that what we wanted and the way we wanted it was not as valid. It's nonsense.

I want to ask you at this point, what do you feel needs to happen for you to take your next step forward? What assistance do you need? What makes you want to do this? What made you want to write something for this book to begin with? I believe that all this discomfort is your inner "call of the wild"-- she wants you to come back home. I am so grateful you have stuck with it and leaned into these uncomfortable places.

I need to meditate more. I need to block everyone out and figure out what I want. I need to write more, and journal more. I need to be questioned and I need help digging into what all of this really means to me.

Yes, you do need to block out everyone else. Ultimately, even me. I can spark something for you (the same way you have done for me in the past), but the real work must be done by you- free from all outside influences. Where we can support each other, we cannot decide or act for each other.

I am confident in my ability to execute a plan, I just want to make sure I have chosen the right plan. My plan starts with finding my true desires as a woman. Who I am and who I want to become. And then ask questions like, "is it okay if the woman I am and the woman I want to become are two different people?" and, "is it okay that something that was a 'yes' for me now, might be a 'no' for me in five years?"

Yes! Of course, that is okay! It is the continual cycle of shedding the old so the new can be born. These are the cycles and seasons of life. It marks growth, expansion, and is the only thing that allows us to remain free. A 'yes' today may be a 'no' tomorrow and that is okay! The important thing is that we are in tune with ourselves enough to hear the change, and brave enough to act on it. This is the practice of acting in personal presence and integrity.

I wanted to write something for this book because you are a beautiful, wonderful woman and I love to be involved in things that you are doing. I am always better because of it and once again, I thank you for all you do.

You are wanted here. I love you. Thank you.

Bailie Holmstead
Artist
BAILIEJAE@GMAIL.COM
@MAKEUPBAILIEJAE

You are wanted here. Your story is wanted here, and I want to leave you with the encouragement to write it down and share it. The stories we tell create the world. If you want to change the world, you need to write and tell your story. Write about what hurts and about what heals. Write about your joy and your sorrow, your love and your loss, your pleasure and your pain. Write what should not be forgotten and then breathe life back into it by sharing it with the world. This is your world. So, record your life. Be conscious of it. Choose it. Create it. Direct it. Rule it. Share it.

For all Wild Women.

Your story....

Your story....

Your story....

Your story.....

Your story....

Your story....

WILD TOGETHER

FOR WOMEN, FROM WOMEN

Brianna's Story

I grew up different than most kids, frolicking in the fields. I was never raised to be like anyone else, I have always been free. I was never schooled in a "proper" manner or forced into religious ideals.

I got to be small and free to play. I learned from nature, since the beginning, this has been my greatest gift. I am not scared to be different, to be too weird, or to be seen.

Life tested me deeply with pain. So I dived deep into plant medicine. I started eating mushrooms when I was 14. The inner freedom I have cultivated as a result of this, is my gift to the world. I have never been afraid to go deep and I have always trusted myself above all else.

Since finding the true love within me, I have learned the nature of reality speaks in miracles and manifestations that further propel us into our alignment. I have learned by honoring myself and my desires that my universe bends its knee to serve me the finest of everything.

Life has always been a ride within Spirit. I've walked to the beat of my own drum since the dawn. The journey back to self love without limits and testing relationships is one that dazzles me forever more. I found my core when I set foot on this green earth and have remembered myself as holy through the intense amnesia that was gifted to me upon arrival.

I realize that I am fortunate to have grown up this way; to have this experience and perspective. If I could share anything with you, it would be this; Be YOU. If you don't know who you are, start fucking yourself. Touch yourself. Make love to yourself. Eat plant medicine and retreat into the Wild. It won't take long to remember your womb, your wisdom and your purpose when you dive into the universal pool that binds the unseen and the seen, the natural and the ethereal. Dive deep, woman.

The truth is, you already do know yourself. You know what you need. You should never question yourself. Follow your pussy pulses and LET GO of everything you second guess. You are infinite. Don't spread yourself thin asking the opinions of others. Look in the mirror, everyone is YOU.

Stop being scared. Stop asking for permission. Do the things you want. Do them if they are in your heart without hesitation & do not let the voices of those who do not roar, silence you. You can do anything and in doing so, you give the chariot to others to rule their own creation.

Brianna Rose

Ascension Medicina
@SORCERESSARTS

'MOONBLOOD' BY MAEVE@WOMANBEART

Encouragement, support, and advice from the @womanbewild @thewomanbecollective Instagram community.

"Woman, Be all of You.

Be too sensitive, too emotional, too dark, and too light. Too sensual, too sexual, too mystical, too much, and too wild. Do not suppress any aspect of your feminine being. Instead, Love and Honor yourself by becoming your own muse. Face your fears by embracing your shadow. Color your true essence into the physical realm by embodying all that you are.
I promise you, what you'll find, will be worth it."

- Maeve
@womanbeart

My soft mossy green heart

Planet to so many emotions

Vibrations

Sensations

Sprouting in kaleidoscopic

Incandescence

Dripping like golden honey down
the eternity of my soul

Mmmm I give this all to my soul family

The love and connection I receive

Experienced for you, in the dream

-Lianna

@womanbepower

'MOODBLOOD 2' BY MAEVE@WOMANBEART

—◦◦∀◦◦—

"You are worthy because you are. There are no requirements or prerequisites. Your worth is inherent. It is internal. It is eternal. It is the same moment to moment. It is the same for every living creature on this planet. It is the same as the brightest star in the galaxy. Your worth is as God's. You are God. I am God. I am you. We are love. We are all one."

—Ember
@womanbebliss

—◦◦∀◦◦—

"A man says a child is born pure and innocent
And that child is good
So why does the same appearance disturb
When She embodies purity
When I am-body my child like innocence
I stand in my truth
In my truth I am shameless

348

I Am

When there's no matter to cover the sacred

To excuse the fact of Being

It's my privilege

To serve you your judgement

It's an honour to expose my tenderness to you

Again and over

Until we may rest in wholeness

Of innocence

For the highest good of all

I release the shame

I evoke our innate right

To wear the skin is a gift

Devotee of Truth,

I surrender"

— Masha
@womanbeinfinite

"You are more than you believe to be real. You are powerful, magical, and infinitely beautiful. You carry whole worlds inside you, with oceans of impossible depth in your eyes, and stardust scattered in shimmering galaxies across your skin. You hold the echo of Great Mother in your blood, bones, breath and womb space. You feel the call of Her drum with every step you take, pulsating through every space inside you when the rest of the world falls quiet. She gave you second sight to guide you, great wings to carry you, and love to keep you strong. Do not let yourself forget that you were meant to lie among mountains and dance with the endless night sky. You were made to shatter gilded cages to fashion crowns for little queens, to remind them they are free from their first breath. This power has always been yours.

Woman, you are more."

− Sâtes
@womanbemagick

"The wolf howls
Our bare feet pound the Earth.
Dirt lines our nail beds,
Our matted hair flys.
We dance the Rhythm of darkness and light,
Birth and death,
Grief and Joy.
Each step a remembrance,
Every sway of our hips is a gift.
We are the women you were taught to fear.
Let our name meet your lips.
Let us show you the wild ways
Come feel your body,
Merge with pleasure.
Be bliss. "

— Victoria
@womanbewitch

"Each and every human being on planet earth has been wired to intuit, your intuition is your compass and it will always point you towards LIFE, it is your true north. Your intuition is your gift from source, it is your communion. Everything you will ever need is already within you, your truest essence is oneness. We are connected, and you are never alone. Never be afraid to flow, never be afraid to let go, and never be afraid to hold on. Simply be, exactly where you are, with your whole heart. Then somehow, you will find that freedom and direction move together, to keep you aligned with your highest purpose. You will experience the dance of the divine masculine, and the divine feminine. Don't forget to dance, and scream, and laugh, and cry. Enjoy your journey with all that you are, feel it all, wild one."

– Jenna
@womanbeflow

"Beautiful woman, this world needs you as you are. Remember to share your love, your gifts, the ability to feel your emotions, to express love and be love. Continue to show up, be too much, love passionately, connect and express your sexuality. Move your body, express yourself and use your voice. Take back YOUR power. This world may not know it yet, but it needs you to break through the shame, guilt, conditions, and control it's tried to suppress you with. You, as a woman, deserve this in your soul. You are worthy of holding space for yourself to feel this, be this, and embody it for yourself. You my love, are worth it, you are seen, you are needed, you are loved, so continue to show up unapologetically. Be YOU!" -

- Jordyn T

"You are effervescent, wild one.
Do not forget that power." -

– Mackey P.

"Community over competition. You will thrive most
when you build up other women."

– Marina W.

"Embrace the unknown. Collaborate with the universe.
Invite, help, and create opportunity. Live your
truth and respect the truths lived by others. Choose
gratitude daily."

–Brooklyn T.

"Your competition is not other women, it's your own inner dialogue that disempowers you."

- Daniella S.

"If your way of expressing yourself is different from those around you, it's okay. It is okay to fiercely as yourself, and also quietly as yourself, just for yourself."

- Jacqueline T.

Fuck it up. Get your hands dirty. Messy action is a REQUIREMENT for personal progression. You cannot wait around for the perfect moment to begin."

- Samantha C.

"Practice self-love every day. BE Love. Know your worth."

— Alexandria D.

"Find What makes you feel strong. Then be strong!"

— Ann M.

"Show up as yourself. Always. It gives others permission to do the same."

— Nichol A.

"It's better to build each other up and support each other for what we are than be jealous of what we think we're not."

– Laura L.

"Build other women up, don't put them down. We aren't each other's enemy."

–Bri W.

"Believe in yourself. You got it, you are worth it, and you are so, so beautiful."

– Noemie F.

"You are of worth, and you belong. "

- Haley L.

"Don't take any moment for granted. Make lists of things you're grateful for. The people in your life are here for a reason, make them aware of how much you love and appreciate them. Look for the best in others and don't let their past stray you from loving them right now. Everyone has good and bad within them. Focus on what's good right now, and forgive the bad. Don't forget what you've been through, but don't hold on to it. You're better because of it. "

- Jessica T.

"Know how powerful you are. Women are healers."

–Tania T.

"Build your own life. Life your dream. You don't need a man to build it for you."

–Mackenzie R.

"Too many people try to say what a "real woman" does or doesn't do. Fuck that."

– Jenna S.

"If there's something you want to do- go for it. More often than not, it will work in your favor."

- Brykelle T.

"It's okay to retrain your mind. Question everything."

- Anavah P.

"Your circumstances do not dictate the potential for who you can be."

- Barbara P.

"Embrace and express yourself without seeking validation from any outside source."

— Shehroz A.

"Do the thing that scares you the most."

— Maria F.

"Lift other women up. We all need to stick together."

— C.Z.

"If you identify as a woman, then you're doing a badass job. Don't let anyone box you in, be wild!"

- Alex J.

"It's okay to be selfish sometimes. It's okay to put yourself first."

- Eleanor H.

"Do not concern yourself with criticism from anyone that you would not request advice."

- Charlotte D.

"You are valuable, even if you don't have 'income'."

- Shelby D.

"Love yourself even when others seem not to."

- Stephanie H.

"Breathe your dreams like air. You're capable of whatever you please. Trust the process."

- Ash X.

―⟨∞⟩―

"Sexuality is a beautiful expression of self. Not your body's default."

- Sierra V.

―⟨∞⟩―

"It's okay to feel things! Being strong doesn't mean not feeling weak sometimes."

- Alynne S.

―⟨∞⟩―

"Become aware of what lights you up and focus your energy on that. We need your magic!"

- Jenn R.

"Love yourself. You don't need a man to be happy."

— Savannah C.

"You don't have to love your whole self every day, but find at least one thing about yourself you do love."

— Fiona M.

"Don't you ever think that you deserve less. You are so worth the very best!"

— Linna S.

"Even when it hurts like hell, draw your shoulders back and open your heart. You are power."

— Savanna L.

"You're a human first, a woman second. This helps reveal what's true and what's societal nonsense."

— Sophie R.

"Trust your heart. It's your strongest compass."

— Callie B.

"Be YOU! The gorgeous badass that you are! Do what makes you happy!"

– Tiffany T.

"There is more to life than chasing after a man, follow your damn heart."

– Cassie T.

"Be your true authentic self and the right things, people, and experiences will find you."

– Kaylee R.

*"You are good enough and deserve to
live your dream life."*

— Jessica N.

*"Be there for one another. Listen and learn,
never assume."*

— Valeria A.

"Lift each other up! We are so powerful together!"

— Kira A.

"Learn to love the other women you see. I love finding something in other women that I love. Their eyes, shape, skin color, brows, anything! Then let them know!"

– Shae J.

"Those that don't lift you up were never meant to be a part of your tribe."

– Jenna D.

"Knowing and loving yourself will always make you a better friend and a better lover."

– Holly F.

"Never be afraid to be yourself."

— Izzy M.

"The way women talk about each other sets the standard for how society treats us."

— Kori P.

"YOU ARE VALID."

— Tiana Z.

"Learn yourself and live your truth."

- Dakota Cheyenne

"Follow your own pleasure as a roadmap to your unique truth."

- Chelsea H.

"See every woman as a reflection of yourself. Love it ALL. The 'beauty and the bith'."

- Seybrielle D.

"Slay your shame! The shame that has been imposed upon you, and the shame you have imposed upon other women. Stop battling one another. Let's be the women who change the energetic shift of the planet. The world needs us!"

- Liz F.

"You, wholly unto yourself, is your greatest source of power."

- Vanessa R.

"Love yourself in ALL your glory before trying to love another person." -

- Suzie M.

"When others instigate or trigger you, respond intentionally instead of reacting impulsively."

– Sharron M.

"Always ask yourself what makes YOU happy above all else."

– Julia R.

"Show and speak more gratitude and compassion for yourself. You are doing a good job."

– Ninja

"Never compare yourself, you are your own queen living in a sea of queens."

– Adriana B.

"Treat yourself the way you treat your best friend- with honesty, support, and love."

– Emily D.

"Be fierce! But also allow yourself to be soft. They're two ends of the same sword."

– Mia S.

‹──◦∿◦❖◦∿◦──›

"Know your worth and never settle for less."

– Kika N.

‹──◦∿◦❖◦∿◦──›

"You are powerful, beautiful, and magical. No matter what."

– Julie A.

‹──◦∿◦❖◦∿◦──›

"You are enough!"

– Nici B.

"Love yourself. And even a little more on the hard days."

- Hannah J.

"Own your power. Be unstoppable."

- Lorin K.

"Loving yourself sets the tone for everything in life."

- Ruxandra B.

"Be exactly who you are. Unapologetically."

—Taye R.

"Touch yourself."

—Tkayah B.

"There is no greater gift you can give the world than loving and honoring yourself first."

—M. Flows

"Look for the goddess in each other."

– Sonja P.

"Be and do whatever you want despite other's opinions"

Arielle K.

*"You are beautiful right now.
Not when conditions are met."*

Cynthia B.

"We share this earth in peace, in harmony, in togetherness."

– Adrianna B.

"You're a strong independent goddess. Don't forget that."

– Annette B.

"Do not give attention to what other people think."

– Heidi E.

⟡

"Identity is something that shifts, flows, and is reinvented with every encounter and experience."

– Anna C.

⟡

"You are the question, you are the answer, and you encompass all the space in between."

– Amanda H.

DETAIL OF SKETCHBOOK

ACKNOWLEDGMENTS

I would like to thank each individual who contributed to the creation of this book. It is true that nothing is accomplished alone.

Master Svietliy, Sak Yant Tattoo Artist, Cover Art

Chiara Mecozzi, Featured Artist, Storyteller

Yarixa Ferrao, Storyteller

Ivy Wolfe, Storyteller

Wendeya Lalla Rose, Storyteller

Brianna Rose, Storyteller

T'Kayah Bell, Storyteller

Christina Mellor, Storyteller

Callie Bishop, Storyteller

Cree Cox, Storyteller

Casey Donaldson, Storyteller

Wendy Zane, Storyteller

Michelle Taggart, Storyteller

Seybrielle Daniels, Storyteller

Jeni Grace, Storyteller

Bailie Hicken, Storyteller

Dan Taggart, Editor

Jennifer Woodhead, Formatter & Designer

SOURCES

Ahmad, Z. (2016). University at Albany, SUNY.

Barczyk, H. (2019). The Lily, Women, Business and the Law 2016.

Ekhator, E. (2015). Women and the Law in Nigeria: A Reappraisal. Journal of International Women's Studies.

Estés, C. P. (1992). Women Who Run With the Wolves. New York, NY: Ballantine.

Martin, R. & Peñaloza, M. (2015). NPR.

McIntyre, J. (2012). Sex And The Intelligence Of The Heart, Rochester, Vermont: Destiny Books.

Naskar, A. (2017). The Bengal Tigress: A Treatise on Gender Equality.

Redden, M. (2017). The Guardian.

Richie, H. (2019). Our World Data: Gender Ratio.

Sjoo, M. (1987). The Great Cosmic Mother: Rediscovering the Religion of the Earth.

State Duma of the Federal Assembly of the Russian Federation: Bill No. 284965-3.

ABOUT THE AUTHOR

- Indigo -

PHOTOGRAPHED BY LIANNA MICHELLE @WOMANBEPOWER

I ndigo is a published author and medicine woman from the Utah desert. She is known for reforming repressive cultural ideas surrounding feminine nature and sexuality through her book, Woman Be Wild, the facilitation of Into The Wild, a group journey of returning to the Wild Self, and her leadership in the Woman Be Collective.

Working as a co-creator with the spirit of plant medicines, she awakens and expands human consciousness and awareness as she gently guides men and women to pursue a path of full sensual freedom by returning to their wild nature.

Indigo currently serves out of her home in Utah as a writing mentor, group course facilitator, plant medicine guide, and body awareness specialist. You can learn more about her and her offerings here;

WWW.WOMANBEWILD.COM

@WOMANBEWILD